Table of contents

Table of contents 1
Introduction to Unit 4A: Crime 3
Study Block 1: Theft, robbery and burglary 5
Chapter 1 Theft: *actus reus* 6
    Appropriation s 3(1) 7
    Property s 4(1) 9
    Belonging to another s 5(1) 10
Chapter 2 Theft: Mens rea 14
    Dishonesty 14
    Intention to permanently deprive 18
Chapter 3 Robbery 22
    Actus reus 22
    Mens rea 25
Chapter 4 Burglary 27
    Actus reus 27
    Mens rea 29
    Summary of the common elements 30
Summary 1: offences against property 33
Study Block 2: Blackmail, fraud, making off and criminal damage 35
Chapter 5 Blackmail 36
    Makes an unwarranted demand 36
Chapter 6 Fraud 42
    Fraud by false representation s 2 42
    Mens rea: 44
    Obtaining services dishonestly s 11 46
Chapter 7: Making off without payment 50
    Actus reus 50
    Mens rea 51
Chapter 8: Criminal Damage 53
    Criminal damage 53
    Mens rea 55
    Destroying or damaging property with intent to endanger life 55
    Arson 56
Summary 2: Blackmail, fraud, making off and criminal damage 60

Study Block 3: Defences 62
Chapter 9 Duress and duress of circumstances 63
    Duress 64
    Self-induced duress 66
    Duress of circumstances 66
    Limits to the availability of the defence of duress 68
Chapter 10 Intoxication 70
    Involuntary intoxication 70
    Voluntary intoxication: Basic and specific intent 71
    The 'Dutch courage' rule 72
    Intoxication and public policy 72
Chapter 11 Self-defence and the prevention of crime 75
    Prevention of crime 75
    Self-defence 75
    Mistaken use of force 77
    Self-defence and intoxication 78
Summary 3: Defences and their effect 80
Examination practice 82
List of abbreviations 90

Introduction to Unit 4A: Crime

My main objective has been to combine legal accuracy with a style that is accessible to all students, so I hope you will find this book both stimulating and helpful. Fully updated with recent cases and laws it is written in a lively, clear and accessible way and is designed to help students of all learning styles to understand the subject.

Although aimed at A-Level the books provide a good base for 1st Year LLB, ILEX and other courses, and can be used as self-study guides.

Each Chapter contains **examples** to help you see how the law relates to real life situations; **tasks** and **self-test questions**, to help you check your understanding, as well as **examination tips** and **application practice** to help you prepare for problem questions. **Summaries** and **diagrams** help to make the law clear and the 'must-know' cases are **highlighted**. Answers are given for the tasks and self-test questions on my website at www.drsr.org

The *'the law explained'* series offers a more in-depth coverage of individual areas with additional tasks, examples and examination practice. This means you can pick those topics for which you need more guidance (all the answers are included in the book).

For a range of free interactive exercises please go to **www.drsr.org** and click on 'Free Exercises' to see what's available.

Unit 4A covers offences against property and the defences to these.

The first Study Block covers *theft, robbery and burglary*. These three offences are very closely connected. Once you have studied theft you will only need a little more for robbery and will also have much of what you need for burglary.

The second Study Block covers *blackmail and fraud*. These offences involve obtaining goods or services in a different way, either demanding something from another person or attempting to gain by some kind of ruse.

The third Study Block covers *making off without payment and criminal damage*. The first offence covers situation like leaving a restaurant without paying and the second is damaging property belonging to another person. This second offence also covers arson.

The final Study Block covers the *defences* of duress and duress of circumstances. These are the defences which are in Unit 4A but not Unit 3A. If you are not studying crime in Unit 3 you will also need to study intoxication and self-defence, so these are included. If you have studied these in Unit 3 you can just use these chapters as revision.

At the end is a chapter with examination practice.

Examination pointer

When studying precedent you learnt that the important part of a case is the *ratio decidendi*, the reasoning behind the judge's decision. As you read a case, think about this and look for the legal principle. Learn to summarise the facts in a few words. This can be valuable when it comes to exams and time is short. Never be tempted to write all you know about an area, you will not be credited for irrelevant stuff even if it is correct.

It is important to:

>   ***explain a case briefly but show that you understand the principle***

show that you understand the law well enough to be selective
DO BOTH!

Study Block 1: Theft, robbery and burglary

Chapter 1: Theft – *actus reus*

Chapter 2: Theft – *mens rea*

Chapter 3: Robbery

Chapter 4: Burglary

This Study Block covers the main three property offences. Theft is a big area so I have split it into two parts. The first two Chapters will cover *actus reus* and *mens rea* respectively. Once you have done theft however, you will find that you have almost all you need for robbery and much of what you need for burglary, which are covered in the following two Chapters.

The terms 'theft', 'robbery' and 'burglary' are used rather indiscriminately in newspaper reports which can be confusing. Simply put, theft covers what most people would think of as stealing, like taking property belonging to someone else without their consent. The offences of robbery and burglary are theft with an added ingredient. Robbery is theft using force, or a threat of force. Burglary is theft from a building.

Example

> I steal a bicycle from outside the railway station. **This is theft.**
>
> I tell the owner I will beat him up if he doesn't give me the bike. **This is robbery.**
>
> I take the bike from someone's back yard. **This is burglary.**

We will look at the different ways a theft may be committed. Although my example is valid, theft is wider than just taking something and can include e.g., merely using something belonging to someone else. Robbery is fairly straightforward but you need to understand what amounts to 'force' so we will discuss this in more detail in the third chapter.

The offence of burglary also includes more than theft from a building. Damaging property can amount to burglary, e.g., so we will also look at the wider issues of this offence in the final chapter of this Study Block.

Chapter 1 Theft: *actus reus*

"... in a prosecution for theft it is unnecessary to prove that the taking is without the owner's consent ..."

Lord Steyn

By the end of this Chapter, you should be able to:

Explain the actus reus of theft

Explain how the law applies in practice by reference to cases

As you can see from the quote, theft is wider than just taking something without permission. It is defined in the **Theft Act 1968 s 1(1)** which says a person is guilty of theft:

'if he dishonestly appropriates property belonging to another with the intention of permanently depriving the other of it'

The offence of theft comes under **s 1**. The following sections then explain each part of the *actus reus* and the *mens rea* in the definition. You will need to learn these too.

Task 1

There are 3 parts to the *actus reus* and 2 to the *mens rea*. Read the definition again and try to identify each of them before going on.

Examination pointer

Giving sections of **Acts** will enhance your answer. One way to remember them is to note that they are in order. **S 1** is the offence itself and then 'dishonestly' **s 2**, 'appropriates' **s 3**, 'property' **s 4**, 'belonging to another' **s 5**, 'with the intention of permanently depriving the other of it' **s 6**. Subsection 1 of each of these explains each term. Further subsections may then add to this.

So you could say "D may be charged with theft under **s 1(1)** of the **Theft Act 1968**. The *actus reus* is the appropriation of property belonging to another. It could be argued here that the items are not property. This is further defined under **s 4(1)** which states ..."

We'll look at each part of the *actus reus* and then the *mens rea*. Did you spot which was which?

The actus reus is

    appropriates s 3 (conduct)

    property s 4 (circumstance)

    belonging to another s 5 (circumstance)

The mens rea is a bit more difficult, it involves

    dishonesty s 2 and

    the intention of permanently depriving the other of it s 6

In this Chapter, we will look at each part of the *actus reus*.

Appropriation s 3(1)

This term covers many more types of conduct than 'take'. It is defined in **s 3** as

'any assumption by a person of the rights of an owner'.

Assumption here means take over e.g., you 'assume' someone's identity if you pretend to be them. For theft, you assume someone's right in property.

The best way to approach this is to consider what rights an owner has in the first place. If you own something, you have a right to do what you like with it. So you can use it, alter it, damage it, destroy it, lend it, sell it, give it away etc. If someone else does any of these things with it then they may well have *appropriated* it because they have 'assumed' your rights.

At one time, it was thought that you could not appropriate something if you had authorisation from the owner, i.e., consent. This caused problems – and much case law.

In **Lawrence 1971**, the HL held there could still be an appropriation even if the owner consented. They found a taxi driver guilty of theft after he took more money than the correct fare (about £7 instead of 55p) from a foreign student. The student had offered him his wallet after he said £1 wasn't enough. He argued it could not be theft because the student gave him the wallet. The House disagreed. The decision was not without its critics. There was an offence under **s 15** of the **Act** of 'obtaining property by deception' which would have covered this type of conduct. Why then, it has been argued, did the House need to interpret **s 3** so widely? The next case appeared to complicate matters further.

In **Morris 1984,** Ds switched labels on goods in a supermarket with intent to pay the lower price. The question was, had an appropriation taken place? The CA held that appropriation took place when D assumed *any* of the rights of the owner, so it occurred as soon as the goods were removed from the shelf with intent to pay the lower price. It could therefore be appropriation even before they switched labels. The HL's interpretation was narrower. Although Lord Roskill said that **s 3** meant interference with *any* of the rights of the owner, he later made clear that there must be 'an *adverse* interference' with those rights'. Thus appropriation only took place when D did something unauthorised (without the owner's consent), in this case, switching labels. In the case of someone swapping labels for a joke, Lord Roskill said that they would have 'appropriated', but would not have the *mens rea* of dishonesty or intent to permanently deprive and so would not be guilty of theft.

So, according to **Morris**, it can be theft even if you don't take anything but there is no appropriation if the owner consents. *Mens rea* may be harder to prove before D gets to the check out, but if, as in **Morris**, you intend to pay less than you should, then you intend to permanently deprive the owner of the difference in price. This is also likely to be seen as dishonest. The HL considered the matter again in the next case.

Key case

In **Gomez 1993**, D was the assistant manager of a shop. He was asked by an acquaintance to obtain some goods in exchange for two stolen cheques. Knowing that the cheques were stolen, D got the shop manager to authorise the sale of the goods to the acquaintance. The CA allowed his appeal against a conviction for theft because the manager had consented. On the basis of **Morris**, there was no appropriation and so no theft. The prosecution appealed to the HL. The appeal raised the question of whether – and how – the earlier two cases could be reconciled. The House decided to revert to **Lawrence**. They held that it was a clear decision that an act could be an appropriation even if done with consent. They declared **Morris** to be incorrect on this point. Lord Keith said that although a customer putting items into a shopping basket is not a thief, the customer has appropriated those items.

So has **Gomez** made the issue certain? Maybe not. In **Galasso 1993,** the same year, the CA seemed to view **Gomez** as not going as far as Lord Keith suggested. Later cases were not always consistent. A narrow interpretation of **Gomez** was seen in **Mazo 1996**. The CA accepted that an appropriation could take place with the owner's consent, but only if that consent had been induced by deception or fraud. In this case, although there was evidence that V did not have full mental capacity, it was held that a gift of a number of cheques she had made to D, her maid, was valid, there was insufficient evidence of any deception. There was therefore no appropriation and D's appeal against her conviction for theft succeeded. However, the next case shows a wider interpretation.

Key case

In **Hinks 1998**, the CA again held that appropriation did not depend on whether there was consent, and said that consent was only relevant to the issue of dishonesty. Here, a man of limited intelligence had been persuaded to give Mrs Hinks, who claimed to be his 'carer', £60,000 over a period of a few months. The CA upheld the conviction for theft. Her appeal was rejected by the HL. Lord Steyn made the point in the opening quote, confirming the *ratio decidendi* of **Lawrence**, and continuing that it went 'to the heart of' the present case. Thus, even a gift could amount to an appropriation. It should be noted that the HL decision was only a 3-2 majority and Lords Hutton and Hobhouse argued strongly that there was no appropriation.

Hinks makes clear that consent is not relevant to appropriation, but is to dishonesty. Thus, the fact that V has consented may be relevant to whether D was dishonest. Otherwise, you could be guilty of theft of a genuine gift. Lord Keith intimated this in **Gomez** when he referred to Lord Roskill's joker in **Morris**. There may be appropriation in such cases, but if it isn't done dishonestly and with intent to permanently deprive then *mens rea* won't be proved. We will look at *mens rea* in the next chapter.

If you come by something innocently but then deal with it dishonestly this can be theft. As we saw, **s 3(1)** defines appropriation as being *'any assumption by a person of the rights of an owner'* it continues *'and this includes, where he has come by the property (innocently or not) without stealing it, any later assumption of a right to it by keeping or dealing with it as owner.'* This would apply if you picked up a mobile phone by mistake, but after getting home decided to keep it.

S 1(2) provides *"it is immaterial whether the appropriation is made with a view to gain or is made for the thief's own benefit"*. This means taking and destroying something is still appropriation. Taking something and giving it away would also come within this section.

Examination pointer

A problem question will usually involve one or two particular issue e.g., it may be arguable whether there is an 'appropriation' or whether the property 'belongs to another'. As I pointed out earlier, **s 1** defines theft. The other sections merely expand on each part of the definition. They aren't offences in themselves. So you should avoid statements like "D will be guilty of appropriation under **s 3**". All 5 elements have to be proved. If they are then D will be guilty of theft under **s 1**. If any one of them can't be proved, D is not guilty of theft.

Task 2

You pick up a watch in a jeweller's intending to steal it. You see a shop assistant looking over at you and put it back. Are you guilty of theft? Jot down whether it has been appropriated and then think about this as you read the other parts of the *actus reus* and *mens rea*. We'll come back to it.

Property s 4(1)

Property includes,

> "money and all other property, real or personal, including things in action and other intangible property"

Real property relates to land; personal would be anything else. Tangible property is something you can touch like a book or a car. Intangible means things you can't touch such as the right to the balance in a bank account or the copyright on a song. These are called 'things in action' because they are rights which can only be enforced by a court action, e.g., by suing someone for stealing the lyrics of a song and making a record. The section goes on to say that (with a few exceptions) land can't normally be stolen. Just about everything else can be though.

In **Kelly 1998**, an artist was given access to the Royal College of Surgeons to draw specimens. He took some body parts and when accused of theft argued it was not 'property'. You can't own someone's body. The CA held it was theft and that parts of a body could come within **s 4** if they had been treated in some way e.g., by preserving them for medical purposes.

In **Marshall 1998,** Ds acquired underground tickets from travellers and then sold them. On appeal, they argued the tickets were not property belonging to another. The CA held that there was appropriation of property (the tickets themselves) belonging to London Underground (who 'owned' them).

In **Oxford v Moss 1978,** an examination paper was taken by a university student prior to the exam. This was not theft of the paper, as he intended to return it. Knowledge of what was on the paper was appropriated, but this was held not to be property.

So, you can steal most things including money and rights. However **s 4(3)** excludes wild plants (unless taken for "reward or sale or other commercial purpose") and **s 4(4)** excludes wild creatures (unless they have been tamed or kept in captivity).

Example

Whilst exercising his rights of access to open land under the **Countryside and Rights of Way Act 2000**, Chris picks some wild mushrooms and then sells them to the local restaurant. He also takes home a rabbit to show his kids. The first is theft because he has taken them for "reward or sale or other commercial purpose". The second isn't unless the rabbit had been someone's pet. In that case, it would also be theft.

Examination pointer

Watch for references to the subsections in a problem question. In my example above you would need to pick up on the fact that although **s 4(1)** includes most things, according to **s 4(3)** you can't normally steal wild plants. Then go on to say it may be 'property' in this case because selling them would be for "reward or sale or other commercial purpose" under **s 4(3)**. As regards the rabbit, this would not be theft if it is wild, but if 'tamed' it can be, **s 4(4)**. Don't worry too much if you can't remember the numbers of all the subsections though – no-one's perfect!

Belonging to another s 5(1)

This is also wide and is not confined to property actually owned by another, having possession or control of it can suffice. **S 5(1)** states,

> 'Property shall be regarded as belonging to any person having possession or control of it, or having in it any proprietary right or interest ...'

Example

You lend a coat to a friend, Sue, for the evening. Whilst she is dancing, someone takes it. They have appropriated property belonging to you, as you owned it. They have also appropriated property 'belonging to' Sue as she had possession at the time.

You can have control of property without knowing of its existence. Thus such property can be stolen. In **Woodman 1974**, the owner of a disused business premises sold a load of scrap metal. He didn't know the buyers had left some behind. D went onto the property and took some of the remaining scrap. He was convicted of theft. The owners of the premises no longer owned the metal, as they had sold it, but they did have 'control' of it.

There is a difference between something which is lost and something which is abandoned. The first belongs to someone so keeping it could be theft, the second does not so can't be.

Example

You have some old books which you don't want anymore. You leave them at college hoping someone may find them useful. You have abandoned them so they cannot then be stolen.

In **Hibbert & McKiernan 1948**, it was held that taking lost golf balls on a golf course was theft. They had been lost, not abandoned.

In **Rickets 2010**, the court considered whether goods left in bags outside a charity shop were 'property belonging to another'. D had argued that they had been abandoned and therefore did not constitute 'property belonging to another'. The court held that if goods were left outside a charity shop then it could be assumed that it was the owner's intention to donate them as a gift to the shop. Therefore, they were not abandoned, but remained the property of the person who had left them until taken in by the charity. Removing the goods before this time could therefore amount to theft. A second point arose as regards control. Some property was also taken from a bin outside another charity shop and the question again was whether it 'belonged to another' The court held that it did, the bin was in close proximity to the charity shop, it could therefore be inferred that the bin was under the control of the charity shop.

It is even possible to steal your own property if someone else has a right to it. **S5** says *'having in it any proprietary right or interest ...'* This is illustrated by **Turner 1971**, where a garage had a right to hold D's car until their bill was paid. Turner was thus guilty of theft when he took it back without paying the repair bill.

Examination pointer

Look out for situations where someone else has possession or control of the property, or where it is debateable whether something has been abandoned and be prepared to discuss these points. Note also that the definition is 'belonging to *another*'. It doesn't say you have to appropriate it from a *particular* person.

Problems occurred where in contract law title to property had already passed, e.g., in **Edwards v Ddin 1976**, D obtained petrol at a self-service station and *then* decided to leave without paying. At the time he appropriated the petrol he had no *mens rea*, when he formed the *mens rea* there was no *actus reus* as title had passed when the petrol entered the tank so it was not 'property belonging to another'. This situation has now been dealt with under **s 3 TA1978**, with the offence of 'making off without payment', which would also apply to leaving a restaurant without paying for a meal if you originally intended to pay. If you intended not to pay from the start it could be theft as you would have the *mens rea* (intent) at the time of the *actus reus* (consuming the food).

Obligation to deal with the property in a certain way

> **S 5(3)** provides, 'Where a person receives property from or on account of another, and is under an obligation to the other to retain and deal with that property or its proceeds in a particular way, the property or proceeds shall be regarded (as against him) as belonging to the other'.

Example

Your mother gives you £20 and asks you to do the shopping tomorrow. You *received* property, the £20. You are *obliged* to *retain* it until tomorrow, and to *deal with* it by doing the shopping. You may have been given the £20, but under **s 5(3)** it *belongs* to your mother.

In **Davidge and Burnett 1984**, D was given money by her flatmates to pay bills. She spent it on Christmas presents. She was found guilty of theft as she had an obligation to deal with it in a certain way (pay the bills) and had not done so.

In **Hallam & Blackburn 1995**, investment advisers were convicted of theft when they did not invest sums entrusted to them. However, there must be an obligation to deal with it in a particular way and thus there was no conviction in **Hall 1973**. A travel agent paid deposits for flights into his firm's account and was later unable to repay the money. He was not guilty of theft as there had been no special arrangements for the deposits to be used in a particular way.

Property received by mistake

S 5(4) provides,

> 'Where a person gets property by another's mistake, and is under an obligation to make restoration (in whole or in part) of the property or its proceeds or of the value thereof, then to the extent of that obligation the property or proceeds shall be regarded (as against him) as belonging to the person entitled to restoration, and an intention not to make restoration shall be regarded accordingly as an intention to deprive that person of the property or proceeds'

Put simply – and it needs to be – this means that if you are given something by mistake (and so have an obligation to give it back), keeping it can be theft. It would cover overpayments of wages as in **AG's Reference No 1 of 1983** where D knew she'd been overpaid and simply left the money in her account. The same applies if you buy goods from a shop and are given too much change by mistake. Essentially the excess belongs to the shop so you are obliged to give it back. Keeping it is theft of that amount.

Task 3

Look at the following situations. Decide if the *actus reus* of theft has occurred and explain the significance of any particular sections in each case.

Sam gets home from college to find she has picked up the wrong coat by mistake. She decides to keep it.

Peter buys a book to read on his journey home and thinks it is such rubbish he leaves it on the train in disgust. Susan picks it up and takes it home.

Simon pays a local builder £100 to buy sand to build a patio. The builder buys himself a second-hand dishwasher instead.

Mary buys a CD and gives a £20 note. She is given change from a £50 note and keeps it.

Summary of theft: S1 Theft Act 1968

Actus reus

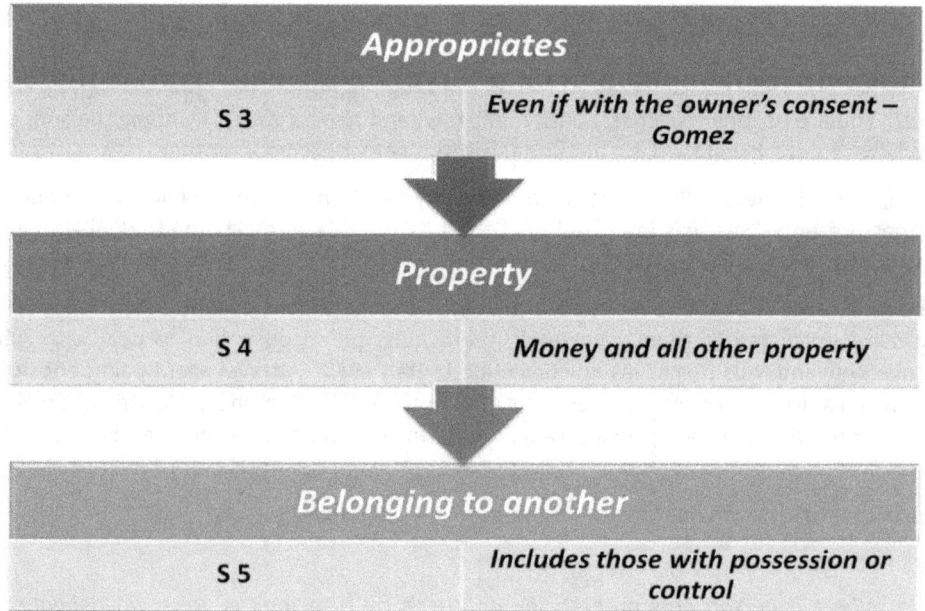

Mens rea (see next chapter) is dishonesty **s 2** and intent to permanently deprive **s 6**

So you may be found guilty of theft in the task concerning the watch. The *actus reus* is the appropriation (by picking it up intending to steal it you have assumed the rights of the owner – **Gomez/Hinks**) of property (the watch) belonging to another (the shop). You also have *mens rea*, you intended to permanently deprive the shop and your actions were dishonest. (We'll look at *mens rea* next.)

Self-test questions

When can wild plants or animals be classed as property?

*Did **Gomez** follow **Morris** or **Lawrence** on the issue of consent?*

From which case did the opening quote come?

*What was appropriated in **Hinks**?*

What are the 2 parts to the mens rea of theft??

For answers to the tasks and self-test questions, please go to my website at www.drsr.org and click the button 'Answers to tasks'. For a range of free interactive exercises, click on 'Free Exercises' to see what's available.

Chapter 2 Theft: Mens rea

"We can see no reason why, when in a jury box, they should require the help of a judge to tell them what amounts to dishonesty"

The CA in **Feely 1971** on the role of a jury

By the end of this Chapter, you should be able to:

- Explain both the actus reus and mens rea of theft
- Explain how the law applies in practice by reference to cases

We saw that theft is defined in the **Theft Act 1968 s1(1)** which says that a person is guilty of theft if,

'he **dishonestly** appropriates property belonging to another with the **intention of permanently depriving the other** of it'

You learnt that 'appropriates' 'property' and 'belonging to another' relate to the *actus reus*. 'Dishonesty' and 'intent to permanently deprive' relate to *mens rea*. Every one of these elements must be proved, or the prosecution will fail.

In **Gomez**, the distinction was made between an honest shopper and a thief. A person who takes an item off a supermarket shelf appropriates it. Only the fact that a shopper means to pay the right price stops them being a thief. This is because they are not being dishonest. They have no *mens rea*. In **Madely 1990**, Richard Madely was found not guilty of theft when he absentmindedly forgot to pay for some goods. The prosecution could not prove *mens rea* because he lacked any intention to permanently deprive.

Dishonesty

The **Act** does not define dishonesty but it does provide three specific situations where the person is *not* deemed dishonest:

S 2(1)(a) provides that a person's appropriation of property belonging to another is not to be regarded as dishonest if 'he appropriates the property **in the belief that he has in law the right to deprive the other of it**, on behalf of himself or a third person.'

S 2(1)(b) provides that it is not dishonest if a person 'appropriates the property **in the belief that he would have the other's consent** if the other knew of the appropriation and the circumstances of it'.

S 2(1)(c) provides that a person is not dishonest if 'he appropriates the property **in the belief that the person to whom the property belongs cannot be discovered** by taking reasonable steps'.

The belief does not have to be reasonable, just *honestly held*. It is subjective, so it is D's belief that is important. However, D will need to persuade a jury that it was honestly held. The less reasonable it is, the harder it will be to convince a jury of this.

Example

You're having coffee with a friend. She goes to the loo leaving her coffee and her handbag on the table. You wait for a while, but need to leave to catch your bus. You drink her coffee and take £50 from her bag (some friend). Can you rely on **s 2(b)**? You'll need to convince a jury that you believe she would have consented in the circumstances. This may not be hard in relation to the coffee; after all it was going cold. It will be a lot harder to convince the jury that you believed your friend would consent to taking the £50 though.

In **Small 1987**, D had taken a car which had been left for over a week with the keys in the ignition. Two issues arose. He argued it had been abandoned and so he believed he had a right to take it – **s 2(1)(a)**. The CA quashed his conviction and made clear that the issue under **s 2** is whether a belief is *honestly* held, not whether it is reasonable. The second issue was not pursued, but if the car *was* abandoned then it did not 'belong to another'. Thus, there would be no *actus reus* and no need to look at dishonesty at all.

Example

You take a bicycle which belongs to a friend. You could argue under **s 2(1)(a)** that the friend owed you money so you believed you had a legal right to it. Alternatively you could argue under **s 2(1)(b)** that you believed the friend would have consented in the circumstances. Under **s 2(1)(c)** you could argue that you thought the friend had left the country and so couldn't be traced by taking reasonable steps.

In a case such as **Small s 2(1)(c)** could also have been argued. Though with a car it would be harder to convince a jury he honestly believed he couldn't trace the owner as cars must be registered.

Note that **s 2** relates to *mens rea* not *actus reus*. So a *belief* that you had a legal right to something is enough, even if you are wrong. Similarly if the other person doesn't consent but you believed they would this will suffice. Lastly, a belief you could not trace the owner by taking reasonable steps would be sufficient. You do not actually have to *take* reasonable steps to find the owner.

Examination pointer

Watch for the above points, especially for **(c)**. It is a common mistake in examinations for candidates to say that as no steps were taken D was dishonest.

The Ghosh test for dishonesty

In addition to **s 2**, which merely shows when D is *not* dishonest, (and despite the opening quote) the courts have developed a test for dishonesty. It comes from the case of **Ghosh 1982**.

Key case

In **Ghosh**, a surgeon claimed fees for operations he had not performed. The question was whether the prosecution had proved that he had acted dishonestly. The CA laid down what is now known as the 'Ghosh test'.

Lord Lane said that the jury must determine whether *"according to the ordinary standards of reasonable and honest people what was done was dishonest. If it was not dishonest by those standards, that is the end of the matter and the prosecution fails. If it was dishonest by those standards then the jury must consider whether the defendant himself must have realised that what he was doing was by those standards dishonest"*.

This means that there are two questions for the jury

> **Was D's act dishonest by the ordinary standards of reasonable and honest people? If not, stop here, if so, ask the second question:**

Did D realise the act would be regarded as dishonest by such people?

If the jury can answer 'yes' to both parts D is dishonest.

As is often the case, it is a two-fold test with both a subjective and objective element. The first, 'objective' test, is what reasonable and honest people would have thought about D's actions. The jury will look at what D did and ask themselves whether they think that action was dishonest. The second, 'subjective' test, is what D believed reasonable and honest people would think. Here the jury will have to decide what *D* was thinking in relation to that action. This is harder, especially where there is a moral element such as Robin Hood stealing from the rich to feed the poor and arguing that he believed reasonable and honest people would not regard it as dishonest.

In **Jouman 2012**, D was convicted of theft after receiving several large cheques from an elderly victim who denied the money had been intended as a gift. D argued the jury should have been directed to the second part of the test, but the CA upheld the judge's decision that she had acted dishonestly as she could not in the circumstances have believed ordinary people would regard her actions as honest.

We saw earlier that **s 1(2)** provides *"it is immaterial whether the appropriation is made with a view to gain or is made for the thief's own benefit"*. This touches on dishonesty as well as appropriation. It means that the Robin Hood argument should fail even though Robin isn't gaining a benefit.

Examination pointer

When discussing the *mens rea* of theft you may need to look at both **s 2** and **Ghosh**. Look for clues in the scenario set, e.g., any reference to being owed money should point you to **s 2(1)(a)**, taking from a friend or colleague to **s 2 (1)(b)**, something found to **s 2(1)(c)**. Reference to D's age or mental capacity requires you to discuss that it is what *D believes* that is important, not what is *reasonable*. If these don't apply, or may not succeed, then explain and apply the **Ghosh** test.

Task 4

Look at the following situations. State which belief under **s 2(1)** you can argue and whether you think you'll convince the jury you honestly held that belief.

- You find a football in your garden and keep it
- You take some money from a friend's bag in an emergency
- You find a £2 coin in the street and keep it
- You find a handbag containing a wallet and credit cards in the street and keep it

Note that under **s 2(2)** the fact that you are willing to pay for the property does not mean you are acting honestly. At first glance, you may think it unfair to find D guilty of theft in such a case but compare the following two situations.

- D takes a bottle of milk from a neighbour's doorstep and leaves more than enough money to replace it
- D is a very rich employer and really likes a vintage car belonging to an employee. One day D takes the car and leaves double what it is worth

In the first situation, you may think it is unfair to find D guilty, but if it weren't for **s 2(2)** the employer wouldn't be guilty either. Anyone could take anything they wanted as long as they could pay for it. Also in the first case D could use the **s 2(1)(b)** defence.

Summary of Dishonesty

Does s 2(1)(a) apply? Belief in a right to the property

Does s 2(1)(b) apply? Belief in consent

Does s 2(1)(c) apply? Belief that the owner can't be found

If the answer is 'Yes', D is not dishonest

If the answer is 'No', apply the Ghosh test

Intention to permanently deprive

S 6(1) provides that this will exist where D's *'intention is to treat the property as his own to dispose of regardless of the other's rights'*.

In **Raphael and another 2008**, D had taken the victim's car by force (robbery) and had then demanded payment for it to be returned. The CA noted that **s 6(1)** included an intention to 'treat the thing as his own to dispose of regardless of the other's rights' and said *"it is hard to find a better example of such an intention"* than an offer to return the property to the owner in return for a sum of money. The return of the property was subject to a condition that was inconsistent with the rights of the owner, i.e., the demand for payment.

It will also exist where property is borrowed *'for a period and in circumstances making it equivalent to an outright taking or disposal'*. This means it is not usually theft if you mean to return the item. This would apply to borrowing but could be different if you have used it and so reduced its value.

Example

You borrow a month's season ticket intending to return it later. You use it for three weeks and are charged with theft. You can argue that you had no intention to permanently deprive the owner of it. This argument is likely to fail. The use of it for this period will make it 'equivalent to an outright taking' and so come within **s 6**.

In **Lloyd 1985,** D borrowed some films from the cinema where he worked and copied them. The CA held **s 6** would apply if D used something so that "all the goodness or virtue is gone". On the facts this was not the case so there was no liability. This narrow interpretation of **s 6** has been seen as rather too generous to D and later cases have shown a significant widening of it.

In **Velumyl 1989**, D took money from his employer's safe intending to return it. The CA held that this was sufficient, as he had treated the money as his own. It was also made clear that as he would be unable to replace the exact notes taken he had intended to permanently deprive the owner of those notes. D's best hope in a case like this is to convince the jury that the intention to put them back showed the conduct was not dishonest.

The broader approach is seen again in **Lavender 1994** and **Marshall 1998**.

In **Lavender**, D took some doors from his flat which belonged to the council. He hung them in his girlfriend's flat which belonged to the same council. Arguably, he hadn't intended to permanently deprive the council of the doors as he merely moved them around. The court held D had treated the doors as his own to dispose of regardless of the other's rights.

In **Marshall**, the CA held that acquiring underground tickets from travellers and then selling them was within the scope of **s 6**. The Ds had treated the tickets as their own to dispose of regardless of London Underground's rights.

Another case which illustrates **s 6** is **Cahill 1993**. Very early one morning D took a pile of newspapers from a newsagent's doorstep on his way home. He was very drunk at the time and couldn't fully explain what he intended to do with them. His conviction was quashed because the judge's direction to the jury only went as far as *'to treat the property as his own'* and did not add *'to dispose of regardless of the other's rights'*. Had the direction been given correctly he may have been found to have *mens rea*. Much would depend on where he dumped them, close by or not. The newspapers would be worthless after the end of the day. If they didn't find their way back to the shop then 'all the goodness or virtue' would be gone.

Examination pointer

If given a scenario like **Velumyl** you could argue that D may not be dishonest under **s 2**. Suggest D may have believed that the owner would have consented (perhaps borrowing from the employer had been allowed before). Or D believed they had a right to it (perhaps they were owed wages). Alternatively rely on the **Ghosh** test. The jury may consider that by intending to return the money, D was not dishonest by ordinary standards.

A final point:

In **Small 1987**, (see below under 'dishonesty') D had taken a car. It may be hard to prove intention to permanently deprive in such a case because a car is easily traceable. Similarly, in **Mitchell 2008**, a car was taken and left only a few miles away and this was held not to be theft as there was no intention to permanently deprive. You should look for clues in the type of property that has been taken. If it would be easy to trace there may be insufficient *mens rea* for theft.

Task 5

Consider the following situations and decide if **s 6** is satisfied:

> Dave takes Steve's tickets for that night's pop concert and returns them the next day.
>
> Frank takes £10 from his mother's purse and puts it in his pocket. His sister sees him and says she will tell if he doesn't return it. He puts it back.
>
> Ellie borrows a book from a friend and reads it. She then throws it away.

Recap

Let's look back at the Task where you took a watch and put it back.

You appropriated (by picking it up) property (the watch) belonging to another (the shop). You have the *actus reus* for theft. Do you have *mens rea*? It may be difficult to find evidence but you know you acted dishonestly. You know 'ordinary reasonable people' would regard the fact that you only put it back because someone was watching as dishonest. You can argue that you didn't keep it so haven't permanently deprived anyone. This actually doesn't matter. It is *intent* to do so that makes it theft. Intent relates to *mens rea* (what you think) not *actus reus* (your actual conduct). Again, it will be hard to prove, but yes, technically you have committed theft. As has Frank in the above task, although he may be able to argue under **s 2(1)(b)**, that he believed his mother would have consented in the circumstances.

Summary – here's the *actus reus* again

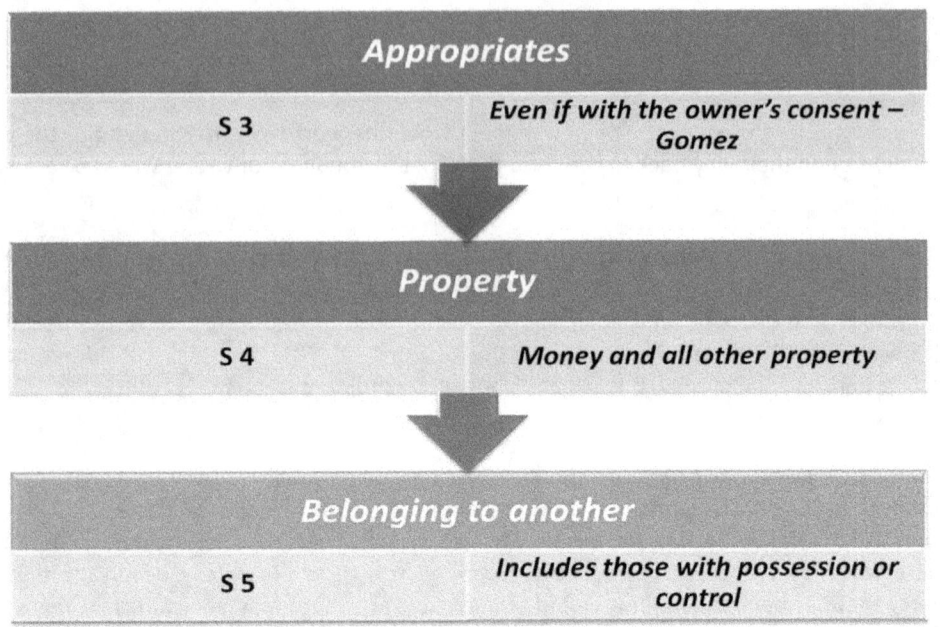

Summary of mens rea

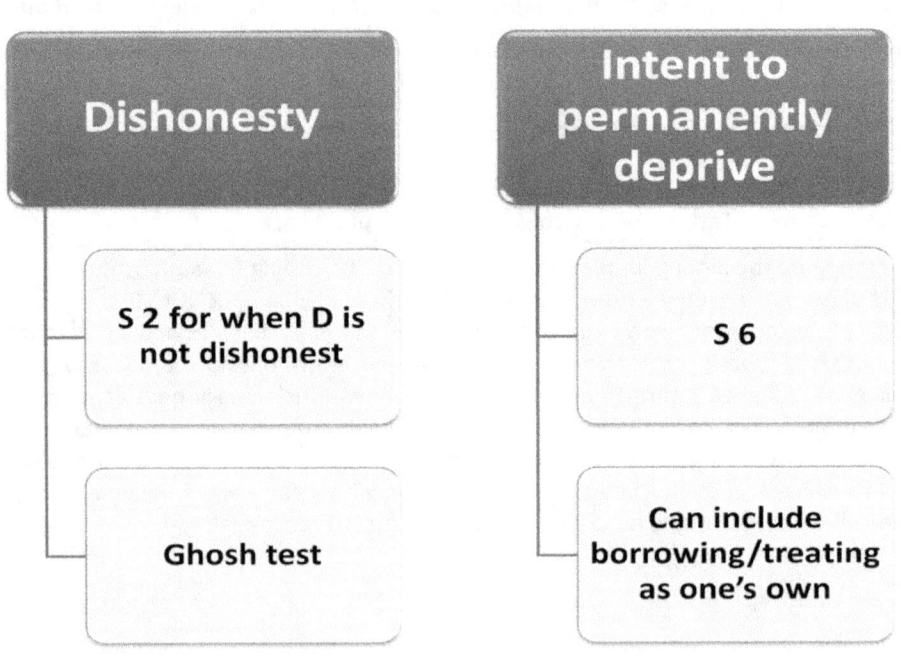

Self-test questions

What are the 3 statutory beliefs in s 2?

Do these beliefs have to be reasonable?

What is the Ghosh test?

When can borrowing amount to intent to permanently deprive?

Can you state all the section numbers dealing with each part of the actus reus and mens rea?

For answers to the tasks and self-test questions, please go to my website at www.drsr.org and click the button 'Answers to tasks'. For a range of free interactive exercises, click on 'Free Exercises' to see what's available.

Chapter 3 Robbery

"What is a robbery, ladies and gentlemen? Well, in very crude terms, it is a theft that has been carried out through violence."

R v West 1999

By the end of this Chapter, you should be able to:

> **Explain the actus reus and mens rea of theft and what turns it into robbery**
>
> **Explain how the law applies in practice by reference to cases**

Robbery is essentially a type of aggravated theft. **S 8** of the **Theft Act 1968** makes it a more serious offence if D uses force (or the threat of force) in order to steal. **S (8)(1)** provides:

"*A person is guilty of robbery if he steals, and immediately before or at the time of doing so, and in order to do so, he uses force on any person or puts or seeks to put any person in fear of being then and there subjected to force*".

It is an indictable offence and carries a maximum life sentence.

Let's look at each part of this offence to clarify what is needed. It's easier than it might look.

Actus reus

There are several parts to this.

> **steals**
>
> **immediately before or at the time of doing so**
>
> **in order to do so**
>
> **uses force on any person or puts or seeks to put any person in fear**

Steals

Robbery involves a theft PLUS the force element. It is therefore necessary to prove all the *actus reus* and *mens rea* elements for theft before considering whether there may be a robbery. An example we looked at with theft is **Raphael 2008**. D had appropriated property (the car) which belonged to another (the owner). He had acted dishonestly and intended to permanently deprive the owner of it (by treating it as his own regardless of the other's rights). He had therefore committed theft. When he took the car, he had hit the man with an iron bar. This turned the theft into robbery.

As you have to prove theft, it follows that you can also use the defences to theft. This means that the **s 2(1)** defences will apply here too. Thus in **Robinson 1977** D threatened V with a knife in order to get money he was owed. He believed he had a legal right to the money (even though he knew he had no right to use a knife to get it) so had a defence under **s 2(1)**. If there is no theft then there can be no robbery.

Task 6

Look back at the *actus reus* and *mens rea* of theft. Be sure you can explain:

Appropriation – property – belonging to another

Dishonesty – intention to permanently deprive

If all these can be proved *and* there is the additional element of force, it may be a robbery.

Immediately before or at the time of doing so

The use (or threat) of force must be before or during the theft. This seems to suggest that the use of force once the appropriation has taken place would not be enough to make it robbery. This is not interpreted too strictly by the courts.

Key case

In **Hale 1979,** the Ds entered the victim's house and one went upstairs and stole some items from a jewellery box. The other was downstairs tying up V. The CA declined to quash their convictions for robbery even though the appropriation may have already taken place. The appropriation was seen as a continuing act. Therefore, it was open to the jury to conclude that it continued whilst the victim was tied up.

In **Lockley 1995**, the court confirmed the point in **Hale 1979** that appropriation was a continuing act. Force on a shopkeeper *after* the D's took some beer could amount to robbery. Remember **Fagan** and continuing acts? No? Then have a look at Chapter 1 again.

Examination pointer

A common mistake is for candidates to go straight on to the robbery issues, but you need a theft to have occurred, so if you see a potential case of robbery in an exam question take it step by step. Firstly, consider whether there is appropriation of property belonging to another. Then consider whether it was dishonestly appropriated with the intention of permanently depriving someone of it. If so, you have theft. Go on to consider if there are any additional elements which may turn the theft into an offence of robbery, as in **Raphael**.

In order to do so

So we can see that the appropriation may continue whilst D is removing the goods from the premises. If force is used, or threatened, this may amount to robbery. However, the force or the threat of force must be 'in order to' steal. This means it must be applied with the purpose of facilitating the theft. If the jury are satisfied that D stole something, yet the force or threat of it was not applied in order to steal, they cannot convict under **s 8(1)**. Using force to get away is not 'in order to steal'. It may be theft, but not robbery.

Uses force on any person or puts or seeks to put any person in fear

The word force is not separately defined in the Act. In **Dawson and James 1978**, the CA said that since it was an ordinary word it was for the jury to determine its meaning. In **West 1999**, the judge made the comment in the opening quote. He then continued, *"What does that mean? What it means, ladies and gentlemen, is; if you are in the supermarket and someone puts their hand into your basket and takes your purse out, a pickpocket, that is theft. It has been stolen from you. If you are outside in the street, and you are approached by someone who held a knife at your throat and then took your purse out of your bag, you will have been robbed, because immediately before or during the course of the theft, you were subject to violence or a threat of violence."* The indication here is that violence is needed, as was the case in **Raphael**. However, it is clear from several cases that the use of force can be small. Snatching a bag from someone's grasp was held to be robbery in **Corcoran v Anderton 1980**. Similarly, in **Clouden 1987**, wrenching a shopping basket from someone's grasp amounted to robbery. However, a really minimal amount of force may not suffice. In **RP v DPP 2012**, snatching a cigarette from someone's hand was held not to be robbery – though it is still theft as property belonging to another has been appropriated.

Examination pointer

As we saw, the full *actus reus* and *mens rea* of theft is required, so any missing element will mean it is not theft and therefore cannot be robbery. On the reverse side of this coin, if there appears to be a robbery but there is insufficient force it can still be theft. Think about it as an equation, if theft + force = robbery, then robbery - force = theft.

A second point arose in **Corcoran**. The two D's had tried to take the handbag by force. It fell from one D's hands and they ran off without it. The court held that the theft was complete when D snatched the handbag from her grasp. This means that a robbery can occur without anything being taken. This isn't as daft as it seems. You can commit theft without taking something. In **Gomez**, it was said that taking something from a supermarket shelf was appropriation. If done dishonestly it could be theft even though you haven't left the shop, if done with force it can be robbery.

Example

You are in a shop. You put an item in your pocket intending to avoid paying for it. You have appropriated property belonging to the shopkeeper. This would be seen as dishonest in the eyes of 'ordinary' people. You would also be intending to permanently deprive the owner of it. This is theft. If you threaten another shopper to "keep quiet or else" when you take it, then you have used the threat of force in order to steal. This is robbery. In both cases, the crime has been committed even if you drop the item in your hurry to get away

Note that the force or threat can be on 'any person'. As in my example, it need not be on the victim of the theft. If you wanted to gain entrance to a casino at night to steal the profits, then knocking out a security guard would suffice. So might tying up and blindfolding someone whose house overlooks the casino. This would depend on why you did it. If it was to prevent them seeing you and raising the alarm it would be robbery. If it was just to prevent them seeing you and pointing you out at a later date it would not. The difference is that in the first case it is *in order to* steal (without being stopped because the alarm has been raised). In the second it is just to avoid being recognised and doesn't help with the theft.

Task 7

Look back at theft to remind yourself of all the parts to the *actus reus* and *mens rea*. Apply these to **Clouden**. You should end up by establishing theft. Keep your workings; we'll come back to this.

Being then and there subjected to force

This means that it must be a threat of immediate force. As with the 'immediately before or at the time' element there is no set time limit. It will be a matter for the jury to decide based on all the circumstances. If the force is used just before or just after (**Hale**) then it may be robbery. However, if D threatens force in a week's time if the security guard doesn't look the other way tonight, it is unlikely to be robbery.

In **R v DPP; B v DPP 2007**, some boys pushed another boy around and took his mobile phone and other items. They were charged with robbery under **s 8**. V said he had not felt particularly scared and the D's argued that as he was not frightened there was no robbery. The court interpreted the Act and held that it was the intention of D rather than the fortitude of V that was important. If this were not the case, guilt would be dependent on how brave, or not, the victim was. This was not what Parliament would have intended and not what the Act implied.

They had intended to scare him and some force had been used so their convictions were upheld.

Mens rea

Firstly, because robbery requires that a theft took place, the prosecution will need to prove the *mens rea* for the theft. This is dishonesty and intention to permanently deprive. If one of these elements is missing it cannot be robbery because there is no theft. In **Zerei 2012**, a conviction for robbery was quashed on appeal because although a car had been taken by force it had been abandoned a very short distance away and was found in about 30 minutes. The judge had not directed the jury properly on the issue of intention to permanently deprive so the conviction was unsafe. On the other hand, this also means D can use the **s 2** arguments to show lack of *mens rea* in relation to dishonesty. In **Robinson 1977**, D had a defence under **s 2(1)** because he believed he had a legal right to the money.

Task 8

Find the notes you made in the last task on **Clouden**. Now add the additional *actus reus* and *mens rea* for robbery. OK? Now you should be able to tackle an exam question.

As regards the robbery itself, accidentally using force or causing fear in a victim is unlikely to be robbery. Robbery requires force 'in order to' steal and accidentally using force would not meet this requirement. Thus, the force or threat of it must be intentional or reckless. As we saw in Chapter 2 all recklessness is now subjective or **Cunningham** recklessness, so D must recognise the risk of force or of putting someone in fear of it.

Examination pointer

You may have a scenario which appears to be a robbery because there is evidence of force. Go through all the elements of theft and then **s 8**. If you then fail to prove robbery on one of the above issues say that although D is unlikely to be convicted of robbery a theft conviction would be possible. The overlap between theft, robbery and burglary means you may need to discuss more than one. Look out for clues as to *how* (force may make it robbery) and *where* (if in a building it may be burglary) it happens.

Summary

actus reus
- steals
- uses force
- or puts someone in fear
- immediately before or at the time

mens rea
- as for theft
- dishonesty
- intent to permanently deprive
- s 2 defences may apply

The final part of the mens rea, applicable to robbery but not theft, is intention or recklessness as to the use of force

Self-test questions

> What turns theft into robbery?
>
> What are the five elements to theft?
>
> How was appropriation treated in **Hale**?
>
> What amounted to force in **Corcoran**?
>
> What is the mens rea for robbery?

For answers to the tasks and self-test questions, please go to my website at www.drsr.org and click the button 'Answers to tasks'. For a range of free interactive exercises, click on 'Free Exercises' to see what's available.

Chapter 4 Burglary

"When you invite a person into your house to use the staircase you do not invite him to slide down the bannisters"

Scrutton LJ

By the end of this Chapter, you should be able to:

Explain the actus reus and mens rea of burglary

Identify the connection with theft and what turns it into burglary

Explain how the law applies in practice by reference to cases

A common view of a burglar is someone sneaking out of a bedroom window late at night with a bag of stolen goodies. This is quite right. Such a person is likely to be a burglar. However, there is – as usual – more to the offence than this.

There are several ways to commit burglary. These come under the **Theft Act 1968 s 9(1)** which has 2 sub-sections.

Under **s9(1) Theft Act 1968** a person is guilty of burglary if:

(a) *'he enters any building or part of a building as a trespasser and with intent to commit any such offence as is mentioned in subsection (2) below; or*

(b) *having entered any building or part of a building as a trespasser he steals or attempts to steal anything in the building or that part of it or inflicts or attempts to inflict on any person therein any grievous bodily harm.'*

S 9(2) Theft Act 1968 provides: *'The offences referred to in subsection (1)(a) above are offences of stealing anything in the building or part of the building in question, of inflicting on any person therein any grievous bodily harm and of doing unlawful damage to the building or anything therein.'*

(NB the original **s 9(2)** included rape but this was removed in 2004).

Actus reus

Much of the *actus reus* is the same for burglary under both (a) and (b). They differ only in the secondary offences, known as the 'ulterior' offences. Under (a), these are theft, grievous bodily harm, or criminal damage. Under (b) they are theft or grievous bodily harm. The main difference between the two is that for (a) D will be guilty without actually committing the ulterior offence. It is enough that the intention to do so is there. In (b) D must commit or attempt either theft or grievous bodily harm (but needn't have intended to do so at the time of entry, we'll come back to this with *mens rea*).

Let's look at the common elements first.

Enters

Both types of burglary require entry as a trespasser. At common law, this included entry by any part of D's body or even an instrument used to remove property. This wide definition seems to have been rejected in **Collins 1972** where the court said entry had to be both 'effective and substantial'.

Key case

In **Collins,** D had had a few drinks. He climbed a ladder to a girl's bedroom and saw her lying naked in bed. He descended, took off his clothes (apart from his socks!), climbed the ladder again and sat on her window sill. She awoke and saw him. The story might have ended there had the girl not also had a few. She thought it was her boyfriend paying a night visit and got up and encouraged him in. They then had sex. At some point, she decided that it might not be her boyfriend. She turned on the light to find that she was right. She slapped him and told him to get out. He was charged with burglary under **s 9(1)(a)**. This meant the prosecution had to prove he entered as a trespasser with intent to rape (which was part of this section until 2004). He argued that he was outside when the girl asked him in so he didn't enter as a trespasser.

His conviction was quashed because the jury had not been properly directed. The CA held that the jury must be satisfied that entry was both "effective and substantial". Edmund Davies LJ said it was not enough that there was trespass at civil law. D had to have known, or at least been reckless as to the fact, that he was trespassing. On these rather unusual facts this was not clear. Had he still been on the ladder when she encouraged him it would not be entry as a trespasser. If he was in the room intending to have sex before this invitation it would be. Sitting on the window sill made it unclear whether he had 'entered' before or after he had been invited. Edmund Davies LJ said *"The point is a narrow one, as narrow maybe as the window sill which is crucial to this case"*.

Later, in **Brown 1985**, the CA said the word 'substantial' was unnecessary. Entry was proved even if D had not fully entered the building. Here D had the top half of his body inside a broken shop window. He argued that there was no entry and so no *actus reus*. His appeal against conviction was rejected.

The CA again considered the issue of entry in **Ryan 1996**. Here D had only his arm and head through a window. Unfortunately for him, he got stuck and had to be rescued by the fire brigade. Again, D's appeal was on the basis that entry was not proved. Again, it was rejected.

A building or part of a building

Note that **s 9** refers to part of a building. This means you may have permission to be in a building – and so not be a trespasser – but not to be in a particular part of it. If you enter that part, you will be entering 'part of a building' as a trespasser. You may therefore be charged with burglary if the rest of the *actus reus* and *mens rea* can be proved. A customer in a shop can commit burglary by going somewhere where customers are not permitted to go. A conviction was obtained in **Walkington 1979**, where D was in a department store and then went behind a counter where he opened a till. The court held that the counter area was a 'part of the building' and he did not have permission to be in that part of the building so had entered it as a trespasser.

In **Stevens v Gourley 1859**, Byles J defined a building as *"a structure of considerable size and intended to be permanent or at least endure for a considerable time"*.

S 9(4) adds that a building includes a vehicle or vessel that is inhabited. Thus, a camper van would be included. It does not have to be inhabited at the time of the burglary.

As a trespasser

Trespass is going somewhere without, or in excess of, permission. Look back at **Collins**. Note that D must be a trespasser at the time of entry.

Example

Susan is invited to a party. She has an argument with the host and is told to go. On her way out she steals a coat. She can't be convicted of burglary under either subsection because she did not enter as a trespasser. Now consider the difference if she had been told to go and then gone into a bedroom and stolen some jewellery. She has entered this part of the building (the bedroom) as a trespasser (she no longer has permission to be there) and can be charged with burglary.

As I said above **s 9** refers to part of a building so if you have permission to be in one part you can still be a trespasser in another part.

Example

In a pub, you are allowed in the bar but not the living quarters. If you went into the living quarters with intent to steal this would be burglary.

Although permission will usually mean there is no trespass it may still be burglary if D goes beyond that permission. In **R v Jones & Smith 1976**, D had left home but had permission to enter his father's house whenever he liked (his father said at the trial "*Christopher would not be a trespasser in the house at any time*"). He came one day with a friend and stole the television. The CA upheld his conviction for burglary. He had gone beyond the permission granted when he stole the television. As he entered with this in mind, he had entered as a trespasser. The opening quote was referred to with approval in this case although it actually came from a civil case. The same could apply to shops where you have permission to be there, but if you enter with intent to steal you have entered as a trespasser.

In **Walkington**, he had argued that he had not entered the shop as a trespasser. The court held that the counter area was a 'part of the building' where customers were excluded. He entered this part as a trespasser.

In **Laing 1995**, D was found hiding in the storeroom of a shop after closing time. His conviction was quashed because at the time he entered the shop it could not be proved he was a trespasser.

Examination pointer

Burglary and theft may come up in the same question so look carefully at the given facts. In my example above, you would discuss burglary and conclude Susan could not be convicted of burglary as regards the coat. She could be charged with theft so you would go on to explain and apply the law on this.

Mens rea

Both types of burglary require entry as a trespasser. Trespass is a civil law concept but for the criminal law, it requires *mens rea*. This is intent or subjective recklessness. You have *mens rea* if you knew or recognised the possibility that you were entering without, or in excess of, permission. This was confirmed in **Collins 1972**. Edmund Davies LJ said there could be no conviction for burglary "*unless the person entering does so knowing that he is a trespasser and nevertheless deliberately enters, or, at the very least, is reckless whether or not he is entering the premises of another without the other party's consent*"

Task 9

Martin is asked by a householder to fit a kitchen. While working in the house he asks to go to the toilet. Once upstairs he sees the bedroom door open and decides to steal some jewellery.

Has he committed burglary and if so which subsection would it come under? Will it make a difference if he doesn't actually take the jewellery?

Summary of the common elements

>Entry as a trespasser
>
>To a building or part of one
>
>With mens rea of intent or recklessness

Once it is proved that D entered a building (or part of one) as a trespasser (knowing this, or being reckless as to it) the *actus reus* and *mens rea* for the ulterior offence(s) must be considered.

Actus reus and mens rea of the ulterior offence

In (a) only *mens rea* is needed. D will be guilty even if none of the ulterior offences is actually committed or attempted. It is enough that the intention to do one of them is there – at the time of entry.

During the riots in the UK in August 2011 there were many looters, and potential looters, who were charged with burglary under **s 9(1)(a)**. As long as D entered a building as a trespasser with intent to steal, a charge of burglary will be appropriate even if nothing is actually taken. In one particular example an estate agent and two 22-year-old students were charged under **s 9(1)(a)** when they were found in PC World outside opening hours. Similarly a youth worker was charged with theft and burglary (entering with intent to steal) when found in possession of a £300 television in Comet. Remember though that the *mens rea* must exist at the time of entry.

Task 10

Look back at **Collins** again. At that time rape was included in **s 9(1)(a)**. At what point did he intend to commit this ulterior offence? If the court had found that he did enter as a trespasser do you think the prosecution would have been able to prove intent for a conviction under **s 9(1)(a)**?

In (b) D must commit or attempt one of the two ulterior offences (so will need both *actus reus* and *mens rea* for the ulterior offence), but needn't have intended to do so when entering.

In **Downer 2009**, the CA confirmed that in order to find out what constituted a burglary, it was essential to have regard to the two types of burglary described in (a) and (b) of **s 9(1)** of the **Theft Act**. The Ds had been arrested while still at the flat they were attempting to steal from, they had therefore committed an offence under **s 9(1)(b)**, i.e., having entered the flat as trespassers, they committed or attempted to commit theft.

Examination pointer

You need to be able to explain the distinction clearly between **s 9(1)(a)** and **s 9(1)(b)**. Examiners' reports often mention this as a failing. For **s 9(1)(a)** D must intend one of the ulterior offences at the time of entry, but need not commit that offence. For **s 9(1)(b)** the ulterior offence must be committed or attempted. So for the first MR is needed before or at the time of entry as a trespasser, and for the second AR and MR is needed but after entry as a trespasser.

Summary of the key issues

> Entry as a trespasser
>
> To a building or part of one
>
> With mens rea of intent or recklessness as to the trespass

Plus

> At the time of entry D has the mens rea of intent to steal, commit GBH or criminal damage for (a) but no further actus reus is needed.
>
> No intent at the time of entry is needed for (b) but actus reus and mens rea of theft or GBH (or attempt) are needed.

Finally, intent to steal only if there is something worth having is enough. You don't need to intend to steal something specific. The CA in **AG's Reference Nos 1 & 2 1979** considered **Husseyn 1977** (a theft case) and held that conditional attempt could be enough as long as the indictment related to theft of unspecified items. In **Husseyn**, the D's had broken into a van containing a holdall with sub-aqua equipment in it. Their appeal against conviction for attempted theft was successful. The indictment had stated intent to steal sub-aqua equipment and as they did not know it was there, they could not be found to have intended to steal it. In **AG's Reference Nos 1 & 2 1979**, the CA did not overrule **Husseyn** but said it only applied where the indictment stated intent to steal something specific.

Example

Dave enters a building intending to steal something only if there is anything of value inside. There isn't anything worth having so Dave leaves empty-handed. This is enough for Dave to be charged with burglary under **s9(1)(a)** – as long as the charge is correctly worded. With intent to steal 'some or all of the contents' would suffice.

Burglary is an either-way offence, tried in either the magistrates' court or the Crown court, unless there is intent to commit GBH in which case it is indictable and can only be tried in the Crown court. The maximum sentence is 10 years or 14 if it is a 'dwelling', e.g., a private house.

Task 11

Look at the following examples and decide if Paul can be charged with burglary. Look carefully at the *actus reus* and *mens rea* and the differences between burglary under (a) and (b). Ask yourself whether he entered with intent or whether he committed the *actus reus* of an ulterior offence. Then decide which subsection these would come under.

Paul comes into your house without permission as he is cold and wants to sleep. He notices a nice clock and takes it.

He again enters because he is cold and wants to sleep but smashes up some furniture to make a fire.

He goes to the house intending to steal but once inside gets scared and runs away.

Summary

Actus reus			S 9(1)(a) and (b)	Mens rea	
Entry	to a building or part of one	as a trespasser		Intent or subjective recklessness as regards the trespass	
S 9(1)(a)				**S 9(1)(b)**	
Actus reus	*Mens rea*			*Actus reus*	*Mens rea*
No further actus reus needed	Intent (to steal, commit GBH or commit criminal damage)			Steals or commits GBH	Mens rea for theft or GBH
	At the time of entry				At the time of the ulterior offence

Examination pointer

If you see that a theft has occurred, look for clues which may indicate it is more than theft. If force is used it could be robbery. If it took place in a building, it could be burglary. Keep an open mind and discuss all the possibilities – as long as they are sensible and relevant to the question.

Self-test questions

> What are the 3 common elements for burglary under both subsections?
>
> What is the mens rea for the above?
>
> What are the 3 ulterior offences for *s 9(1)(a)*?
>
> What are the 2 ulterior offences for *s 9(1)(b)*?
>
> At what time does mens rea have to exist?

For answers to the tasks and self-test questions, please go to my website at www.drsr.org and click the button 'Answers to tasks'. For a range of free interactive exercises, click on 'Free Exercises' to see what's available.

Summary 1: offences against property

Theft s1 Theft Act 1968 s3		appropriation
s4	actus reus	property
s5		belonging to another
s2	mens rea	dishonesty
s6		intent to permanently deprive
Robbery s8	actus reus	Theft PLUS force or the threat of it in order to steal
	mens rea	As for theft
Burglary	actus reus for both types of burglary	entry to a building or part of one as a trespasser
s 9(1)(a)	mens rea – no further actus reus needed	with intent to steal, inflict GBH or cause unlawful damage
s 9(1)(b)	actus reus – no further mens rea needed	steals or inflicts GBH, or attempts to do so

Task 12

Note the principle and brief facts for the cases below

- *Gomez*
- *Woodman*
- *Ghosh*
- *Clouden*
- *Hale*
- *Collins*
- *Jones & Smith*

Concepts connections

Morals

Will a jury be able to ignore the moral element if D has acted in a morally acceptable way? (**Ghosh**)

Justice

Justice appeared to be done in Lawrence but then Morris confused the issue. Gomez restated Lawrence but later cases again conflicted. Justice cannot be done if there is uncertainty in the law. It does not seem just that for robbery the use of force can be really minor yet the maximum sentence is life imprisonment. (**Corcoran/Clouden**)

Fault

The low level of fault where force is very minor can be used here too (**Corcoran/Clouden**). This can be compared to theft which requires a high level of fault as the mens rea is intent

Balancing conflicting interests

The subjective element in s 2 Theft Act 1968 attempts to balance property rights with D's rights by providing that D may argue a belief even if it is not reasonable (**Small**)

Study Block 2: Blackmail, fraud, making off and criminal damage
Chapter 5: Blackmail

Chapter 6: Fraud

Chapter 7: Making off without payment

Chapter 8: Criminal damage

This Study Block covers the other property offences. For the first three offences, the emphasis is on how property or services are obtained. The first is where a demand is made in order to receive money or other property. The second involves two different offences. These are fraud by false representation, where D gives false information or a false impression with intent to gain, and obtaining services dishonestly, where D doesn't obtain property but receives a service without intending to pay for it in full. The third offence is making off without payment. This is where the property or service has already been obtained but then D decides not to pay for it. The final offence is slightly different. Criminal damage is where property is not taken but damaged or destroyed; this offence also covers arson – where the damage or destruction is by fire.

Examples

Tom tells Tim that if he doesn't pay him £1,000 he will beat him up. This is blackmail. Tom has demanded money with menaces.

Tom points a gun at Tim and tells him to give him his car. This is also blackmail. Tom has demanded property with menaces. Note the overlap with robbery; this would also be committing theft with the use or threat of force.

Sara applies for a job using a false reference which shows she previously had other jobs of the same nature. This is fraud by false representation as she has falsely represented her employment record in order to obtain a job – and a salary.

Sara uses a fake student card to get a discount at art exhibition. This is obtaining services dishonestly as Sara has received a service (seeing the exhibition) without paying in full.

Mike goes out for a meal and having eaten it he leaves without paying. This is making off without payment.

Mike goes out for dinner and is so disgusted with the meal that he throws it on the floor, breaking the plate into pieces. This is criminal damage as he has damaged the plate, the food – and possibly the floor! If he set fire to the tablecloth in his rage this would be arson.

Chapter 5 Blackmail

"In our judgment it is only rarely that a judge will need to enter on a definition of the word 'menaces'. It is an ordinary word of which the meaning will be clear to any jury" Lord Lane

By the end of this Unit you should be able to:

Explain the actus reus of blackmail

Explain the mens rea of blackmail

Understand and use the cases which illustrate the various elements of blackmail

The offence of blackmail comes under **s 21(1) Theft Act 1968**. This provides that a person is guilty of blackmail

"if, with a view to gain for himself or another or with intent to cause loss to another, he makes any unwarranted demand with menaces"

The *actus reus* is:

> **makes an unwarranted demand**
>
> **with menaces**

The *mens rea* is:

> **with a view to gain for himself or another or**
>
> **with intent to cause loss to another**

Let's look at the *actus reus* and *mens rea* in more detail. First the *actus reus*.

Makes an unwarranted demand

There are two parts to this, the demand itself and the fact that it is unwarranted.

Demand

A demand can take many different forms, and although usually the demand is for money or other property **s 21(2)** provides that "the nature of the act or omission demanded is immaterial". The demand may therefore be for something other than money or other property, although this may not be as wide as it seems because the view to gain or intent to cause loss must be of money or other property, we'll come back to this later with *mens rea*.

Example
Pete threatens Dave, saying 'give me a job or I'll beat up your sister'. This is as much blackmail as saying 'give me £100 or I'll beat up your sister'. Look at the elements required, in both cases there is a *demand* 'give me a job/give me £100' with *menaces* 'I'll beat up your sister'. Under **s 21(2)** it does not matter that the first demand is not for money or other property because "the nature of the act or omission demanded is immaterial". As regards *mens rea*, in both examples D has a view to gain money from the demand, a wage from the job or £100.

Can a demand be made in a letter? If so when is it made, on posting or on receipt? The following case deals with this issue.

Key case
In **Treacy v DPP 1971** D wrote and posted a letter in England addressed to a woman in Germany. He demanded that she send £175 to him in England under the threat that if she did not he would send her husband photos of her with another man. The issue was whether he

could be tried in England, but in deciding that he could, the HL made the point that if a demand is contained in a letter then that demand is made as soon as the letter is posted. There were also *obiter dicta* to the effect that if a demand with menaces "*goes astray and never reaches the addressee, or reaches him but is not understood by him, or because of his unusual fortitude fails to disturb his equanimity*" then, although that may affect the punishment, it is still blackmail.

This means that D can be guilty of blackmail even if the other person has not heard the threat or has heard it but is not intimidated in any way. The demand is complete once made, it does not have to be communicated. On the other hand, the CA held in **Hester 2007**, that the demand could be a continuing one and did not cease until payment. One of the grounds for appeal was that although blackmail had occurred (a man was imprisoned and held to ransom) D's involvement did not occur until after the threat was made. The CA disagreed and held that even where all of the ingredients of blackmail are present before a person's involvement, the blackmail continues until the demand ceases and the threat is withdrawn. D became involved during that time so was also guilty of the offence.

Unwarranted

According to **s 21 (1)** a demand is unwarranted unless the person making it does so in the belief

"(a) that he has reasonable grounds for making the demand; and

(b) that the use of the menaces is a proper means of reinforcing the demand"

This is subjective. It is not what a reasonable person may believe, but whether this particular D believes that there are reasonable grounds for making the demand *and* that using menaces is proper. It will be for the jury to decide whether D believed it was both reasonable and proper, so much will depend on the evidence and the circumstances. If, for example, D was owed money the jury may be persuaded that D believed the demand was warranted. Although a matter for the jury, there may be occasions where it is clearly an unwarranted demand. This would be the case where D knew the threatened act was unlawful.

Examination pointer

Students frequently make the mistake of saying that for a demand to be warranted D must have reasonable grounds for making it and the use of menaces must be a proper means of enforcing it. This is not the case; it is that D must *believe* the grounds for making the demand are reasonable and the use of menaces proper. Make sure you are clear on this point.

Key case

In **Harvey, Ulyett and Plummer 1981**, the Ds had paid a man £20,000 for what was supposed to be cannabis but wasn't. Angry at being swindled they kidnapped his wife and child and threatened to harm them if the money was not returned. The judge said a threat to perform a serious criminal act could never be a proper means of reinforcing a demand within s **21(1)** and D appealed that this was a misdirection. The CA agreed it was a misdirection and confirmed that **s 21(1)** was concerned with the belief of the individual defendant in the particular case and what a reasonable person may believe was irrelevant, so it should have been left to the jury to decide whether the Ds had actually believed their demand was proper. However, no act which D believed to be unlawful could ever be believed to be proper, even if D believed it to be justified. The correct direction should be that '*the demand with menaces was not to be regarded as unwarranted unless the Crown satisfied them that the defendant had not made it in the genuine belief that he had reasonable grounds for doing so and that the use of the* menaces was in the circumstances a proper, meaning lawful, means of reinforcing the demand'.

Both parts of **s 21 (1)** need to be satisfied so even if D had (or believed in) a right to the property demanded, this may satisfy the first part, but if the means used to enforce that right is not proper (or, according to **Harvey**, not lawful) then the second part fails and D will be guilty of blackmail. In **Vine v Waltham Forest LBC 2000**, the CA indicated that wheel-clamping may come within blackmail if the amount demanded for unclamping the car was exorbitant. On the facts it was held to be reasonable so there was no blackmail.

S 21(2) further provides that it is "immaterial whether the menaces relate to action to be taken by the person making the demand". Thus 'give me £100 or my friend Bob will beat up your sister' will suffice.

With menaces

It is the need for 'menaces' that makes the demand criminal. A demand may be quite unthreatening but can be turned into blackmail by an added threat. "I'd be really grateful if you gave me £50" doesn't sound like blackmail, and isn't as it stands, but add "if you don't I'll beat you up" and things change somewhat. The Criminal Law Revision Committee proposed the word 'menaces' as it was felt to be stronger that 'threats' and therefore restricted the offence. Thus in **Harry 1974**, during a student rag week, shopkeepers were offered immunity from 'inconvenience' in return for donations to charity. This was held not to be sufficient 'menace'. It is clear though, that it does not need to be a threat of harm or injury, we saw in **Treacy** that the threat to send the husband the photographs was sufficient. In **Weddell 2007**, D threatened his uncle that if he did not give him £150,000 he would tell the police, his family and the world, about the sexual abuse which he had suffered as a child while on holiday with his uncle.

It was stated in **Clear 1968** that whether the demand is with 'menaces' depends on whether the mind of 'an ordinary person of normal stability and courage' would be sufficiently influenced or made so apprehensive as to do what D demands. This is a matter for the jury but in **Garwood 1987** the CA said it would not normally be necessary to direct the jury on the meaning of menaces. Here D had threatened a rather timid person into giving him £10. The question was whether there was sufficient menace. Lord Lane made the opening quote but continued that there may be occasions a direction to the jury was needed. This would be where the threats might have affected the mind of an ordinary person of normal stability but did not affect the person actually addressed (there would be a sufficient menace), or where the threats had in fact affected the mind of the victim, but would not have affected a person of normal stability (there *could* be a sufficient menace but only if D knew the likely effect of his actions on the victim).

On the facts it was apparent that D knew the effect his threats had on the victim so blackmail was proved. So, it is what D does and knows that matters, not the effect on the victim. The essence of the offence of blackmail is the demand, the result is immaterial. In **Strachan and McGuigan 2008**, unreported, two men had tried to sell tapes containing allegations of a minor royal being involved in sex and drugs to various newspapers. When they failed to sell the story they demanded £50,000 from the royal instead. However, he contacted the police, eventually leading to the involvement of SO15, the anti-terrorist organisation. Even though the royal had not paid the money demanded, the jury at the Old Bailey took less than five hours to find them guilty of demanding money with menaces.

Examination pointer

Watch for the overlap between other **Theft Act** offences and blackmail, also with the defence of duress. In **Raphael 2008**, D had taken the victim's car by force and had then demanded payment for it to be returned. On the facts this was robbery but blackmail could be an alternative if, for example, it was difficult to prove an intention to permanently deprive or if the threat was not 'in order to steal'. You may need to discuss more than one offence.

Examples

I beat you up in order to take your car. This is robbery.

I beat you up in order to take your car and demand payment for its return. This is robbery and may also be blackmail if sufficiently menacing.

I take your car from outside your house and demand payment for its return. This is not robbery (no force in 'order to steal'). It may be blackmail and will also be theft if there is an intention to permanently deprive.

Task 13

Match the cases to the principles

Treacy 1971

Weddell 2007

Hester 2007

Harvey, Ulyett and Plummer 1981

Garwood 1987

It is the belief of the individual D in the particular case not what a reasonable person may believe that is important in deciding whether a demand is unwarranted

Menaces only needs explaining if V is not affected, or is affected and a normal person would not be

The demand need not be communicated

The demand may be a continuing one

The threat does not need to be a threat of harm or injury

Now let's look at the *mens rea* elements. We'll take them together because the rules are the same for both.

With a view to gain or intent to cause loss

There are two alternative parts to the mens rea, although they often go together because a view to gain for oneself or another will usually mean an intent to cause loss to someone else. View seems wider than intent and indicates that the gain or loss need not be expected immediately. The gain or loss must be of money or other property but can be temporary. This is specifically provided for in the interpretation section of the Act. **S34 (2) (a)** provides that 'gain' and 'loss' are to be understood as *"extending only to gain or loss in money or other property, but as extending to any such gain or loss whether temporary or permanent"*. A demand for a loan would therefore amount to blackmail if made with menaces.

Whether it is a gain or a loss, remember that this relates to *mens rea*, not *actus reus*, so no gain or loss need actually be made. It is similar to theft, where there must be an 'intent to permanently deprive' but there is no need for D to actually deprive anyone of anything. The main point of s34 is that D must be making a demand with a view to gaining money or other property. Once a demand is made, with sufficient menace and with *mens rea*, then the offence is made out even if no property is actually gained or lost.

Example

Look at the following threats.

'I'll shoot you if you don't inject me with this drug'.

'I'll shoot you if you don't have sex with me'.

'I'll say you had sex with me if you don't give me £50 to keep quiet'

Can you see which would be blackmail and why? In all three there is a demand with menaces, but what about *mens rea*? I have a view to gain in each (the drug, the sex or the £50) but is this a view to gain property? The first is, as I acted with a view to gain a drug, which is property. However in the second there is no property, so it is not blackmail. The third will be blackmail because the view is to gain money, the sex here relates to the demand (*actus reus*) not the gain (*mens rea*).

N.B. The first example is similar to **Bevans 1987** where D pointed a gun and demanded that a doctor inject him with morphine, a painkiller.

Although the words 'view to' imply something in the future, it is clear that D can have a view to gain something already held. **S34 (2) (a)** continues

"(i) "gain" includes a gain by keeping what one has, as well as a gain by getting what one has not; and

(ii) "loss" includes a loss by not getting what one might get, as well as a loss by parting with what one has"

This could apply where D threatens another into foregoing a £50 debt, for example. There is a view to gain ('by keeping what one has', the £50 borrowed), also the other person is losing the right to be paid ('by not getting what one might get', the £50 owed). Note, though, that there is no need for *both* a gain and a loss, one or the other will do to.

One final thing on the *mens rea*, the **Act** refers to gain or loss for or to 'another' so the gain or loss can be that of a third party. A demand with menaces to a person to give someone else £50, (a view to gain for another) or a demand that a person destroys someone else's property (an intent to cause loss to another) will suffice.

Examination pointer

As well as considering other offences, as mentioned above, watch also for a possible defence of duress. A demand by Jim that John must rob a shop and hand over the proceeds would be blackmail by Jim, but could also be theft, burglary or robbery by John with a possible defence of duress. Be very careful to read the question to ensure whose liability you are asked to discuss.

Task 14

Before looking at the summary write down the definition of blackmail. Now pick out each part of the *actus reus* and *mens rea*. Try and find a case or a section of the statute that adds to each of these elements. When you have finished use the summary diagram to check what you have done, then write it up on a card and keep it for revision.

Summary

D is guilty of blackmail under **s 21 (1)** if, *"with a view to gain for himself or another or with intent to cause loss to another, he makes any unwarranted demand with menaces"*

actus reus	makes an unwarranted demand	with menaces
Treacy v DPP 1971	The demand is complete once made, it does not have to be communicated	
Hester 2007	the demand can be a continuing one and does not cease until payment	
s 21 (1) a demand is unwarranted unless the person making it does so in the belief:	(a) he has reasonable grounds for making the demand (b) the use of the menaces is a proper means of reinforcing the demand	
Harvey, Ulyett and Plummer 1981	it is clearly an unwarranted demand where D knew the threatened act was unlawful	
mens rea	with a view to gain for himself or another	with intent to cause loss to another
s 34 (2) (a) (i)	"gain" includes a gain by keeping what one has	
s 34 (2) (a) (ii)	"loss" includes a loss by not getting what one might get	

Self-test questions

What does s **21(2)** provide?

What is the point made in **Treacy v DPP 1971**?

When might it be necessary to direct the jury on the meaning of 'menaces'?

In which case was this confirmed?

What are the two alternative parts to the mens rea?

For answers to the tasks and self-test questions, please go to my website at www.drsr.org and click the button 'Answers to tasks'. For a range of free interactive exercises, click on 'Free Exercises' to see what's available

Chapter 6 Fraud

"The offences broadly fell into two categories, that is to say offences in which the Applicant solicited contracts for building work, obtained a cash deposit but in respect of which nothing was done. The second group were where he solicited investment funds from others, in effect asking for £633 on the basis it would in due course produce £1,000, whereas perhaps inevitably it produced nothing".

Hedley J

By the end of this chapter you should be able to:

> Explain the actus reus and mens rea of fraud by false representation under s 2
>
> Explain the actus reus and mens rea of obtaining services dishonestly under s 11
>
> Use examples to illustrate both offences

Fraud by false representation s 2

S 1 creates a single offence of fraud which can be committed in three ways. One way is under **s 2(1)**, fraud by false representation. This is committed when a person:

"(a) dishonestly makes a false representation, and

(b) intends, by making the representation–

(i) to make a gain for himself or another, or

(ii) to cause loss to another or to expose another to a risk of loss"

The *actus reus* is:

> **making a representation**
>
> **that is false**

and the *mens rea* is:

> **dishonesty (in making the representation) and**
>
> **intent to make a gain or to cause loss**

Let's look at *actus reus* first.

Making a representation

The representation can be as to fact or law, and includes a representation as to the state of mind of either the person making the representation or any other person. It can also be express or implied. This is stated in **s 2 (4)**. Thus, it can be written or spoken, posted on a website, or be communicated by conduct. An example of a representation by conduct is given in the government guidelines to the **Act** where, for example, a person dishonestly uses a credit card to pay for items. This is falsely representing that the person producing the card has the authority to use it. In **Lambie 1981** D used her credit card after the bank had withdrawn its authority to do so. She was convicted under the old law, but this would now be making a false representation. The implied representation would be that she had the authority to use it, and this was false. Other types of conduct could be wearing a false identity tag or a fake uniform. A representation by omission will also suffice, for example not correcting a false impression that you are someone else, or leaving out a relevant fact on an application for a job or mortgage loan.

That is false

The Act describes a representation as false as being one where:

"(a) it is untrue or misleading, and

(b) the person making it knows that it is, or might be, untrue or misleading"

It is clear from the Act that you can make a representation to a machine. **S 2 (5)** provides:

".... a representation may be regarded as made if it (or anything implying it) is submitted in any form to any system or device designed to receive, convey or respond to communications (with or without human intervention)"

This means that fraud can be committed where a person enters someone else's details when using a cash machine, or a chip-and-pin machine in a shop. Under the old offences there had to be a deception of a person. You could not deceive a machine (although it could have been theft) only a human being. Now entering someone else's details when using a cash machine will be an offence under **s 2**. This leads to another point, the offence is complete once the false representation is made, the effect on the person to whom it is made is irrelevant.

Example

Susan logs on to Tesco's on-line shopping service and orders £40 worth of food and drink, using a credit card she found in the street. She has implied that she has authority to use the card, which is untrue, and also she knows this to be untrue. She is therefore making a false representation. Mind you, if she gives her own address for delivery she's also pretty daft!

Had Susan used the card in the actual store and the cashier did not believe her so refused to serve her, this is still an offence of making a false representation. The effect on the cashier is irrelevant, the offence is complete once she makes her false representation.

These are the facts from **Lambie 1981**. D used her credit card to obtain goods from a branch of Mothercare, but she had already exceeded her credit limit on the card. Under the old law much depended on whether the shop assistant had been induced by the representation to part with the goods. The judge held D had committed an offence by falsely representing that she was authorised to use the credit card to obtain the goods. The CA disagreed and held that the shop assistant was not induced by this, since the state of D's credit with the bank did not concern the shop. The HL held that on the presentation of the credit card D was representing that she had authority to make the contract with the shop and that the bank would honour the voucher. This induced the assistant to complete the transaction, as she would not have done so had she known there was no authority. D was guilty. The new law will be easier to apply because the question of whether a shop assistant was induced by the representation will be irrelevant.

An example since the **Fraud Act** is where a manager at Tesco's used his company credit card to pay for a music festival, of which he was the director. The festival had lost money and he had started using the card to pay the debts. The amount totalled £355,000 and he was convicted of theft and fraud by false representation. He had dishonestly appropriated the funds with intention to permanently deprive Tesco of the money and this amounted to theft. He had also falsely represented that he had the authority to use the card to this extent so was guilty of fraud by false representation

Another example is where an IT programmer working for Sainsbury's was convicted of theft at the Old bailey in December 2010 after stealing loyalty scheme points from Nectar.

Whilst he was working at Sainsbury's he created a number of false accounts into which he credited 14 million Nectar points, worth over 73 thousand pounds. At 2 points for each pound spent in the supermarket he would have had to spend around £7 million in order to earn that number of Nectar points. He had dishonestly appropriated the points, which had a monetary value and he had the intention to permanently deprive the supermarket of this amount. He also admitted fraud by false representation. This was in respect of redeeming £8,120 of the points for grocery shopping. This is similar to a person dishonestly using a credit card to pay for items. The person producing the card is falsely representing they have the authority to use it and here he falsely represented that he had the points to use in exchange for the groceries.

Examination pointer
Be clear on the fact that there is no need for the representation to be acted upon. The offence is centred on what D does, not the effect on V. If you are given a situation where a false representation is made but no-one takes any notice don't make the mistake of saying D is not guilty. The offence is complete once the false representation is knowingly made.

The representation must be made knowing it is, or might be, untrue or misleading. Thus D must be aware of the fact that what is 'represented' is, or might be, either untrue or misleading.

In February 2011 three hospital workers were convicted after pleading guilty to fraud by false representation. They had used false UK Border Agency stamps in their passports to obtain work. They had falsely represented that they had the authority to remain and work in the UK, knowing that representation to be false.

Although knowledge comes under the description of false in the Act it is essentially a *mens rea* matter. The other parts of the *mens rea* are dishonesty and intent.

Mens rea:
The *mens rea* requires both dishonesty and intent:

> *dishonesty in relation to the making of a false representation and*
>
> *intent in relation to making a gain, causing a loss or exposing another to the risk of loss*

Dishonesty
This will be decided in the same way as for theft. That is, by using the test set out in **Ghosh**, which asks two questions:

> *whether the defendant's behaviour would be regarded as dishonest by the ordinary standards of reasonable and honest people, and, if so,*
>
> *whether the defendant was aware that his / her conduct would be regarded as dishonest by reasonable and honest people.*

If the answer to the first question is 'no' then there is no further question and the defendant should be acquitted. However, if the answer is 'yes' the second question should be asked.

Intent to make a gain or cause a loss

There must be an intent to make a gain for oneself or another, or intent to cause loss to another or to expose another to a risk of loss. Note that it is *mens rea* not *actus reus* so it is the state of mind of the defendant that is important. There is no need to make a gain or cause a loss, just to intend to do so. **S 5** defines 'gain' and 'loss' as any gain or loss of money or other property, whether temporary or permanent, including intangible property such as copyright. This is similar to theft. Gain includes "a gain by keeping what one has, as well as a gain by getting what one does not have", and loss includes "a loss by not getting what one might get, as well as a loss by parting with what one has." This is the same as for blackmail (under **s 34**

Theft Act 1968) and similar to theft, where keeping something can amount to an appropriation.

In **Fiander 2016**, (unreported) a woman gave a false reference in order to obtain a job. She had knowingly made a false representation (providing a false and misleading reference) with the intention of making a gain (her earnings from the job) and ordinary people would regard doing so as dishonest. This was an express representation of fact (and was false and misleading) so she was guilty under **s 2**.

In a parliamentary question session in June 2007, several questions were asked of the government in relation to offences under the **Fraud Act 2006**. The questioner gave the following hypothetical examples and enquired whether an offence under the **Act** would have been committed in the circumstances and, if so, under which section:

a bailiff repeatedly charges for work that has not been done

a person represents himself to be a certificated bailiff, but is not, and by doing so obtains a payment or goods from a debtor

a person represents himself to be a certificated bailiff, but is not, and intends by so doing to obtain a payment or goods from a debtor

The government spokesperson confirmed that in all three situations the offence would be fraud under s 1 by means of false representation as set out in **s 2**. Specifically, "*a bailiff or any other person who dishonestly charges for work that has not been done will be committing an offence under the Fraud Act 2006*". So anyone who charges for work, and then does not do it may be liable under **s 2**. This was the case in **Davies 2008**, from which the opening quote came. Here D had preyed on elderly people, in some cases asking for deposits for building work which was never done, and in others asking for money for investments, which were never made. In many cases he accompanied them to a cash machine to ensure they gave cash deposits. He was found guilty of 22 charges under **s 2**.

Regarding the second example, in particular the *mens rea*, the spokesperson said, "*It will be necessary to show that the person was acting dishonestly in making the false representation, as well as that they intended to make a gain or cause a loss. It is immaterial whether they actually obtained a payment or goods from a debtor.*" The final example was also said to come under this section. Note that, as the government spokesperson said above, there is no need for any actual gain or loss to be made.

A modern problem that will be caught by **s 2** is 'phishing'. This occurs where someone pretends to be a bank or other business (a dishonest representation) and sends out bulk e-mails with the intent to 'catch' some of the recipients (intending to make a gain or cause a loss). This is done by directing them to what appears to be a genuine website which asks them to register details such as bank account or credit card numbers. With this information the sender can gain access to the person's bank account or purchase goods using that person's identity.

Task 15

Alice used her credit card to buy some clothes from a shop, but she had already exceeded her credit limit on the card   Apply **s 2** to these facts and decide whether Alice will be found guilty of fraud by false representation.

Obtaining services dishonestly s 11

The other **Fraud Act 2006** offence that you need is that of obtaining services dishonestly. Under **s 11 (1)** an offence is committed if a person *"obtains services for himself or another -*

(a) by a dishonest act, and

(b) in breach of subsection (2) "

Under **s 11 (2)** a person obtains services 'in breach of subsection 2' if:

> **they are made available on the basis that payment has been, is being or will be made for or in respect of them**
>
> **they are obtained without any payment having been made for or in respect of them or without payment having been made in full and**
>
> **when they are obtained the person**
>> knows they are being made available on the basis described in (a) or
>>
>> that they might be, but
>>
>> intends that payment will not be made, or not made in full

Essentially, there must be a dishonest act and then subsection 2 comes in. This requires that the services are provided on the basis that payment will be made at some point, whether past, present or future, and that D knows this and intentionally does not pay, or does not pay in full. Let's break this down a bit.

Actus reus

There are three parts to this, the latter two of which come under subsection 2:

> *obtaining services by a dishonest act (S 11 (1))*
>
> *on the basis that payment will be made (S 11 (2))*
>
> *without such payment being made either in full or in part (S 11 (2))*

The first point to note is that a dishonest *act* is required, this means that, unlike **S 2**, the offence cannot be committed by an omission. Also unlike **S 2**, a service must actually be obtained for the *actus reus* to be complete.

Examination pointer

You may need to discuss both **Fraud Act** offences. In many cases of obtaining services dishonestly, D will also have committed an offence under **S 2** of the **Act**, fraud by making a false representation, the representation being that payment for the services will be made. Note carefully that **s 11** requires the obtaining of the service to actually occur. This differs from **s 2** where there is no need to actually make a gain or cause a loss, just to intend to do so. Look for clues as to whether something has been gained or lost. This may help you decide what the most appropriate charge is.

Services are described as those which are made available on the basis that payment will be required at some point (past, present or future). The service must therefore be chargeable to fall within **S 11**. In relation to e.g., banking services, free services will be excluded. If a service is obtained for which payment is expected at some point, and that payment is either not made at all or is only made in part, then the *actus reus* is satisfied.

Mens rea

There are also three parts to this, and again the latter two come under subsection 2:

Mens rea is satisfied if a person:

> *obtains the services by a dishonest act (S 11 (1)) and*
>
> *knows the services are made available on the basis that payment has been, is being or will be made, or that they might be (S 11 (2)) and*
>
> *intends that payment will not be made, or will not be made in full (S 11 (2))*

So, the *mens rea* again involves the **Ghosh** test for dishonesty and proof of intent, as with **s 2**. Dishonesty in relation to the obtaining of the service, and intent that payment will not be made, or not be made in full. However for this offence the defendant must also 'know' the services are made available on the basis that they have been, are being or will be, paid for. The offence is therefore committed if services for which payment is expected are obtained by a dishonest act without payment being made, or not being made in full (*actus reus*), where D knows such payment is expected and intends not to pay in full (*mens rea*).

Example

John finds a season ticket in the street and uses it to gain entry to a football match. He has obtained services, watching the match, and he will probably be seen as dishonest as he knows he has no right to use the ticket. He also knows that watching the match is something that should be paid for and he intends not to pay. He has both *actus reus* and *mens rea* for **s11 Fraud Act 2006.**

Several examples are given in the guidelines to the **Act**, these include:

> *a person climbs over a wall and watches a football match without paying the entrance fee*
>
> *a person dishonestly uses false credit card details or other false personal information to obtain Internet data or software where the service is only available to someone who has paid for access rights to it.*

In the first instance a **s 11** offence will be committed because the service, the football match, is made available on the basis that it will be paid for, and climbing over the wall is pretty good evidence that the person is acting dishonestly and intends not to pay. Under the old law an offence would not be made out because the provider of the service has not been deceived (unlike John using a stolen season ticket to enter the grounds where the ticket collector would be deceived, which could come under both the new and the old law).

In the second instance a person is committing a **s 11** offence by giving false details to obtain the provision of data or software knowing payment is expected, and intending not to pay for it. Giving false details would indicate dishonesty and intent not to pay, and it is probable that the user would know that payment is expected or they would not have bothered to give false details.

Other examples are given in the CPS guidelines on the Act. These include where D:

> *orders a meal in a restaurant knowing he has no means to pay*
>
> *attaches a decoder to his TV to enable him to access chargeable satellite services without paying*
>
> *uses the services of a members' club without paying and without being a member*

Task 16

Look back at the chapter on theft. Make a note of the *actus reus* and *mens rea* elements under the **Theft Act**. Now compare to **s 2** and **s 11 Fraud Act**. In particular note the differences so you would be able to apply the law appropriately in an exam question.

So, a final reminder, don't treat these offences in isolation, note the overlap not only between the two **Fraud Act** offences, but also with theft. The fraud offences may be easier though, because there is no need to prove that property belonged to another, nor an intention to permanently deprive.

Examination pointer

In an exam you should consider alternatives where appropriate. Look back at the previous example. **S 2 Fraud Act** is also a possibility as John made a false representation, that he has the right to use the ticket. However, it may be hard to prove intent to gain property or cause another to lose it, as the ticket has already been paid for, so the club won't lose, and he has gained a service by his representation, not 'money or other property'. So go on to consider theft, there is a possible charge under the **Theft Act 1968** in relation to taking the season ticket, but there could be a problem with proving intent to permanently deprive. Has 'all the goodness' gone (**Lloyd**)? John could argue that the ticket was abandoned and so not property belonging to another, but this is likely to fail (**Hibbert & McKiernan**), or he could use **s 2** to say that that he believed the owner could not be found so he is not dishonest, although on the facts this is unlikely to convince a jury.

Summary

S 1	creates a single offence of fraud	*actus reus*	*mens rea*	examples
S 2	fraud by false representation	making a false representation	dishonesty and intent	charging for work not done
	there is no need actually to make a gain or cause a loss, just to intend to do so			using false chip-and-pin details
				phishing
S 11	is a separate offence of obtaining services dishonestly	*actus reus*	*mens rea*	
	this **does** require the obtaining of the service actually to occur	obtaining services on the basis that payment will be made without such payment being made either in full or in part	dishonesty, knowledge and intent	climbing a fence to watch a football match
				using a stolen credit card
				using a decoder dishonestly

Self-test questions

What is the actus reus for s 2?

*How does **S 5** define 'gain' and 'loss'?*

*What were the facts in **Davies 2008**?*

Which of the two offences cannot be committed by omission?

*What is the mens rea for **s 11**?*

For answers to the tasks and self-test questions, please go to my website at www.drsr.org and click the button 'Answers to tasks'. For a range of free interactive exercises, click on 'Free Exercises' to see what's available

Chapter 7: Making off without payment

"(making off) may be an exercise accompanied by the sound of trumpets or a silent stealing away after the folding of tents" Court of Appeal in Brooks & Brooks

By the end of this Unit you should be able to:

Explain the actus reus and mens rea of making off

Explain how the law applies in practice by reference to cases

The **Theft Act 1978 s3** provides:

'*a person who, **knowing that payment on the spot for any goods supplied or service done is required or expected from him, dishonestly makes off without having paid as required or expected and with intent to avoid payment** of the amount due*' shall be guilty of an offence.

This covers a variety of situations which, for some reason, may fall outside the other property offences. An example is leaving without paying for petrol or a meal. The property doesn't belong to another for theft (because it is now mixed with your own petrol or stomach contents!). It is for this reason that the 1978 **Act** introduced this new offence.

Let's take the various parts of the actus reus and mens rea in turn.

Actus reus: Makes off, without having paid as required or expected

Mens rea: Knowing payment on the spot is required, dishonesty and intent to avoid payment

Actus reus

Makes off

In **Brooks & Brooks 1983** the CA held that makes off meant 'depart'. There is no need to run away. They also indicated that the 'spot' was the 'place where payment is required'. This would include a cash desk. The opening quote came from this case.

In **McDavitt 1981** D was not liable under s3 when he refused to pay a restaurant bill after an argument with the manager. The 'spot' was held to be the restaurant itself. He had not yet left the restaurant, so had not made off from the spot.

Compare the following cases:

In **Troughton v MPC 1987** the CA quashed D's conviction on the basis that payment was not yet 'required on the spot'. D was drunk. He asked a taxi driver to take him home. He couldn't remember exactly where he lived and they had an argument. The taxi driver took him to a police station where he ran off. He had made off, but not from the spot where payment was 'required'.

Another taxi case was **Aziz 1993**. Here there was another dispute about the fare. When the 2 Ds refused to pay, the driver started to take them to the police station. They became disruptive and he pulled up. They ran off but D was caught and arrested. He argued that he had not made off from the spot where payment was required. The CA held that the 'spot' could be in the taxi itself or even outside it. There was no need for a specific location. S3 was satisfied.

Without having paid as required

Payment cannot be 'required' if the goods or services supplied are contrary to the law. This could include drugs or stolen goods. It can also cover situations where the payment is not legally enforceable because it isn't yet due, as in **Troughton**.

Mens rea

There are 3 parts to this.

> *D knows that payment is required on 'the spot'*
>
> *D is dishonest*
>
> *D intends to avoid paying*

Knowing payment is required on 'the spot'

If D believes the goods or services are on credit then there may be no offence. Also if D believed that someone else was paying.

Example

You get a taxi back from the office Christmas party. You haven't any money so can't pay when the driver asks for the fare. You thought the taxi journey was on account and a bill would be sent. Alternatively you believed that your employer was paying for transport home for all staff. In neither case do you 'know payment is required on the spot'. You have not committed an offence.

In **Vincent 2001,** D successfully argued that he had an agreement to pay his hotel bills at a later date so could not know that payment was required on the spot.

Dishonesty

This is a matter for the jury. The normal **Ghosh** rules will be applied. Note however that D won't be dishonest if there was a genuine reason for not paying.

Example

I order a meal in a restaurant. When it eventually arrives I eat a few mouthfuls but it is cold and inedible. I refuse to pay for it and leave. This will not be making off as the mens rea is not proved. I have not been dishonest.

Intends to avoid paying

It must be show that D had no intention of *ever* paying. A temporary intention is not enough.

Key case

In **Allen 1985,** D left his hotel without paying the bill. He argued that he intended to pay as soon as a business deal matured. The HL interpreted s 3 to mean D intends to avoid paying *permanently*. They held that the question of whether D intended to avoid payment permanently was one for the jury to decide, and quashed his conviction.

Task 17

Look back at my earlier example of getting a taxi home from the office party. What if I realised the office wouldn't pay but I intended to send the money at the end of the month when I got paid? Explain what I might argue and whether it would relate to *actus reus* or *mens rea*.

Examination pointer

Note the overlap with fraud. Look carefully at the given facts and the timing of any representation e.g., as to paying for a meal. More than one offence may therefore need to be explained and applied. If D orders a meal intending not to pay then the Fraud Act is appropriate. Both s2 and s11 because there is an implied representation that the meal will be paid for and the serving of the meal has been obtained dishonestly. If D orders a meal and later decides not to pay then making off without payment will be the appropriate charge.

Summary

Actus reus

    D makes off from the spot (Brooks)

    Without paying as required or expected (Troughton)

Mens rea

    D knows that payment on the spot is required (Vincent)

    D is dishonest (Ghosh)

    D intends to avoid payment permanently (Allen)

Self-test questions

    What are the 2 parts to the actus reus under s3?

    What are the 3 parts to the mens rea under s3?

    Why was D guilty in **Aziz** but not in **Troughton**?

For answers to the tasks and self-test questions, please go to my website at www.drsr.org and click the button 'Answers to tasks'. For a range of free interactive exercises, click on 'Free Exercises' to see what's available

Chapter 8: Criminal Damage

"it is unnecessary to establish such definite or actual damage as renders the property useless, or prevents it from serving its normal function" Walters J

By the end of this Unit you should be able to:

Explain the actus reus and mens rea of the criminal damage offences

Distinguish between the basic and aggravated offences

Explain how the law applies in practice by reference to cases

The **Criminal Damage Act 1971 s1** covers 3 offences:

criminal damage s1 (1)

criminal damage with intent to endanger life s1 (2)

arson s1 (3)

Arguably there are 4 offences as arson may also be with intent to endanger life. There is, however, no separate section for this. It would be both **s1 (2)** and **s1 (3)**.

Criminal damage

S 1 (1) provides

'A person who without lawful excuse destroys or damages any property belonging to another intending to destroy or damage any such property or being reckless as to whether any such property would be destroyed or damaged shall be guilty of an offence'

OK. Let's break the offence down a bit.

Actus reus

destroys or damages

property

belonging to another

without lawful excuse

Destroys or damages

This covers more than you might think. In **Samuels v Stubbs 1972**, Walters J said it was difficult to lay down any general rules about what would amount to damage. He said much would depend on the particular circumstances, the type of property damaged and how it was affected. He then continued with the opening quote. In **Hardman v Chief Constable of Avon & Somerset Constabulary 1986,** members of CND used water-soluble paints on pavements to depict vaporised humans in a protest to mark the 40th anniversary of the dropping of the Hiroshima bomb. This would easily wash away. However their conviction was upheld as the council had been put to the expense of cleaning the pavements. This can be compared to **R v A (a minor) 1978** where D spat on a policeman's overcoat and was found not guilty on the grounds that the spittle could be easily removed with a damp cloth.

It would appear to be criminal damage if someone is put to the expense of repairing or cleaning. In **Fiak 2005**, D had blocked the toilet in his prison cell with a blanket which caused flooding. This amounted to criminal damage because the blanket and cell had to be cleaned.

It will not amount to criminal damage if there is no impairment to usefulness or value. In **Morphitis v Salmon 1990** a scratch on scaffolding was held not to amount to criminal damage as it did not impair the usefulness or value of the property.

Property

The definition is similar to that for theft but there are slight differences. Obviously you cannot damage intangible property, so this is excluded. Wild creatures which have been tamed or are ordinarily kept in captivity are included, but mushrooms, flowers, fruit or foliage of a plant growing wild on any land are not.

Belonging to another

The property must belong to another. As with theft this is wider than just ownership. It includes another having custody or control of property, having a right in property or having a charge on it. It is not an offence to destroy your own property. Also if you *believe* you are destroying your own property you will have a defence. The belief does not have to be justifiable as long as it is honestly held.

In **Smith 1974** some tenants had damaged floorboards and panels when removing wiring which they had installed with the landlord's permission. However the wiring had become part of the fixtures of the flat and they had no right to take it. Their conviction was quashed on appeal. The CA held that no offence is committed if a person damages property "in the honest though mistaken belief that the property is his own, and, provided that the belief honestly held, it is irrelevant to consider whether or not it is a justifiable belief.'

Example
I break up the dining-room furniture to put on the fire because I have run out of firewood. I am not guilty of an offence as the furniture was mine. It turns out one of the chairs belonged to my lodger. If I did not realise this then I am still not guilty of an offence, as I honestly believed this was also mine.

Without lawful excuse

In addition to the general defences there is a special defence of lawful excuse in s 5(2) (a) and (b). This does not apply to criminal damage endangering life though.

Lawful excuse is where D destroys or damages property in the belief that:

> *the person entitled to consent would have consented to the destruction or damage if they had known of it and its circumstances (s 5(2) (a)) or*

> *it was necessary in order to protect property belonging to himself or another which he believed was in immediate need of protection and he believed the means adopted were reasonable, having regard to all the circumstances (s 5(2) (b))*

Essentially there are 2 defences here, belief in consent and protection of property. A few cases will help to explain how they work.

First 5(2) (a)

In **Jaggard v Dickenson 1981** D was drunk and broke into a house thinking it belonged to a friend. She believed her friend would have consented to the damage caused. In fact it was the house of a stranger and the magistrates held that she could not rely on the defence because she was intoxicated. This was reversed on appeal. It was held that her defence should based upon her belief and her drunkenness did not invalidate this.

In **DPP v Blake 1993** a vicar used a marker pen to write a biblical quotation on a wall outside Parliament. He was protesting about the Gulf war and argued the consent defence. In this case he claimed he had God's consent! He failed. The court held that nothing within the meaning of the **Act** covered consent by God.

Now s 5(2) (b)

In **DPP v Blake 1993** the vicar also tried to rely on 5(2) (b). He claimed he was protecting the property of the people of the Gulf States. His defence failed on the grounds that the people of the Gulf States were too far away to benefit from his actions, therefore s5 (2) (b) was not applicable.

In **Chamberlain v Lindon 1998**, however, D successfully relied on s5 (2) (b) when he demolished a neighbour's wall. He believed it blocked his right of access to his own property. He had an honest belief that his property rights needed immediate protection and that the means adopted were reasonable, having regard to all the circumstances.

Mens rea

The *mens rea* is:

> *intention to destroy or damage property belonging to another or*
>
> *recklessness as to whether such property is destroyed or damaged*

Note that recklessness is now subjective recklessness. This comes from **Gemmell & Richards 2003**. The HL overruled their own decision in **Caldwell 1982** where they had held that the mens rea for criminal damage was objective recklessness. This is no longer good law. The question now would be whether D recognised the risk of damaging or destroying property (and of endangering life for the aggravated offence).

Key case

In **Gemmell and Richards 2003** 2 boys aged 11 and 13 set light to some papers outside the back of a shop. Several premises were badly damaged. They were convicted of arson on the basis of **Caldwell** recklessness, i.e. whether the risk of damage was obvious to a reasonable person. Their ages were therefore not taken into account. They appealed. The CA cannot overrule a decision of the HL and their argument under the Human Rights **Act** also failed. They made a further appeal to the HL which used the **1966 Practice Statement** to overrule its previous decision. The HL held that the **Caldwell** test was wrong and that the *defendant* had to have recognised that there was some kind of risk.

Examination pointer

Criminal damage may well come up with a question on theft or one of the related offences. Look out for things like "D broke into the house to steal something". Burglary will be the obvious crime but a discussion of criminal damage in relation to the breaking in can earn extra marks. Unless, that is, the question specifically asks you to discuss only offences under the Theft **Act**. As always, read the question carefully.

Destroying or damaging property with intent to endanger life

This is often referred to as aggravated criminal damage.

s 1 (2) provides that

"a person who without lawful excuse destroys or damages any property, whether belonging to himself or another -

a) *intending to destroy or damage any property or being reckless as to whether any property would be destroyed or damaged; and*

b) *intending by the destruction or damage to endanger the life of another or being reckless to whether the life of another would be thereby endangered;*

shall be guilty of an offence".

This is similar to criminal damage but with the addition that D intended or was reckless with regard to endangering life. It is a much more serious offence. The maximum sentence is life imprisonment.

Here the damage does not have to be to property belonging to another. However the 'lawful excuse' defence under **s 5 (2)** does not apply as it is specifically excluded by **s 5(1)**.

Example

I set fire to my house so I can claim on the insurance. This would not be an offence under **s 1 (1)** and **s 1 (3)** but if I knew there were people inside I could be convicted under **s 1 (2) and s 1(3)** and I would not be able to rely on **s 5**.

Note the words 'intending *by the destruction or damage* to endanger the life of another'. In **Steer 1987**, D was convicted under s 1 (2) when he shot at the window of a former business partner. His appeal was successful. The HL held that the danger to life had to come from the destruction or damage of the property. It was not enough that it resulted from the original action (firing shots).

In **Stringer 2008**, the CA confirmed that the test for intent is the same as it is for murder i.e., the two-part test from Woollin.

> *whether it was a virtual certainty that somebody would suffer death or serious injury in these circumstances*
>
> *whether D appreciated this*

In this case, D started the fire using accelerant, and knew several of his family were sleeping upstairs. At the time he was 14 and had a low IQ. However, even taking account of his age and low IQ, the jury had found both parts of the test satisfied. The convictions for both murder and arson with intent to endanger life were upheld on appeal to the CA.

However, in **Farnon 2015**, several young people had started a fire in a derelict building which had spread to a pile of tyres. This caused noxious fumes which filled several rooms, killing a homeless man who was sleeping there. The CA confirmed that the Ds must have subjectively appreciated both the risk of fire and the risk of endangering life. They had not realised the tyres would catch fire and cause the lethal fumes so were guilty of arson under **s 1(3)** but not of arson with intent to endanger life under **s 1(2)**.

There does not necessarily have to *be* a danger to life. It is enough that D realised that life would be endangered.

Example

I cut the brake cable on someone's bike because I have a grudge against the owner. I know that life will be endangered as soon as it is ridden. As it happens the owner has just got a new bike. The old one is taken apart for spares and never ridden. I have not actually endangered life – but I intended to do so. I am guilty of aggravated criminal damage.

Arson

s 1 (3) provides

"An offence committed under this section by destroying or damaging property by fire shall be charged as arson"

This is also regarded as a very serious offence. The maximum sentence is life imprisonment. It is criminal damage as above under s 1 (1) or s 1 (2) but if the damage was caused by fire it "shall be charged as arson". Thus there can be arson contrary to s 1 (1) and s 1 (3) – the basic arson offence, or arson contrary to s 1 (2) and s 1 (3) – the aggravated offence. An example of the latter is **Stringer**, discussed above.

In **MPC v Caldwell 1982,** D was convicted of arson when he set fire to a chair in the hotel where he worked. Although the fire was put out before anyone was harmed he had endangered the lives of the residents. This would therefore be arson contrary to s 1 (2) and s 1 (3).

In **Elliot v C (a minor) 1983,** a 14-year-old girl with low intelligence was convicted of arson. She had set fire to a neighbour's shed. She had poured white spirit over the floor and set fire to it to get warm. This case was decided on the old test for recklessness. This meant it did not matter that she did not recognise the risk. A reasonable person would have seen the risk and this was enough. Since **Gemmell** the test is subjective recklessness. Under this test she would have had no *mens rea*.

The lawful excuse defence can be used here too. Thus in **Denton 1982,** D set fire to his employer's mill and successfully argued that his employer had consented to this in order to make a fraudulent insurance claim. However, as noted above, it cannot be used where there is intent to endanger life.

Summary
The basic offence s1 (1)

Actus reus	Mens rea	Defences
• damaging or destroying • property • belonging to another	• intent or subjective recklessness • as to whether property belonging to another is damaged or destroyed	• belief in consent • belief the property needs protecting • general defences

The aggravated offence s1 (2)

Actus reus	Mens rea	Defences
• damaging or destroying • property • (need not belong to another)	• intent or subjective recklessness • as to whether property is damaged or destroyed and • as to endangering life	• general defences only

Arson s 1 (3)

Actus reus	Mens rea	Defences
• damaging or destroying • property • belonging to another • by fire	• intent or subjective recklessness • as to whether property belonging to another is damaged or destroyed	• belief in consent • belief the property needs protecting • general defences

Task 18
Look at the summary of the offences. Make a note of the differences and add a case example for each. Keep this for revision.

Self-test questions

Does damage have to be permanent?

What is the mens rea of the basic offence?

*What changed in **Gemmell**?*

What is the lawful excuse under s5 (2) (a)?

Does D's belief have to be reasonable for s 5?

For answers to the tasks and self-test questions, please go to my website at www.drsr.org and click the button 'Answers to tasks'. For a range of free interactive exercises, click on 'Free Exercises' to see what's available

Summary 2: Blackmail, fraud, making off and criminal damage

The main thing in an examination is to be able to accurately state the law and then apply it to the specific facts given. This means being able to explain the appropriate terms with the relevant offences as well as the correct section numbers.

Here is a summary of the four offences with the relevant statute and sections you need to know.

Blackmail comes under **s 21(1) Theft Act 1968** and is an unwarranted demand with menaces. The MR is 'with a view to gain for himself or another or with intent to cause loss to another'

Under **s 21 (1)** a demand is unwarranted unless the person making it does so in the belief

"(a) that he has reasonable grounds for making the demand; and

(b) that the use of the menaces is a proper means of reinforcing the demand"

Under **21(2)** it is "immaterial whether the menaces relate to action to be taken by the person making the demand".

S34 (2) (a) provides that 'gain' and 'loss' are to be understood as *"extending only to gain or loss in money or other property, but as extending to any such gain or loss whether temporary or permanent"*.

Fraud is of two types which come under s2 and s 11 of the Fraud Act 2006

S2 is fraud by false representation.

Under **s 2 (4)** it can be express or implied

S 2 (5) provides that the representation need not be made to a person

S 5 defines 'gain' and 'loss' as any gain or loss of money or other property, whether temporary or permanent

S 11 is obtaining services dishonestly

Under **s 11 (1)** an offence is committed if a person *"obtains services for himself or another -*

(a) by a dishonest act, and

(b) in breach of subsection (2) "

S 11 (2) adds

    on the basis that payment will be made

    without such payment being made either in full or in part

Making off comes under the **Theft Act 1978 s3**

This section covers both the AR and MR.

AR is making off from the spot without paying as required or expected

The MR is knowing that payment on the spot is required, dishonesty and intent to avoid payment permanently.

Criminal damage comes under s 1 of the Criminal Damage Act 1971

The AR of the basic offences is:

> *destroys or damages*
>
> *property*
>
> *belonging to another*
>
> *without lawful excuse*

The MR is:

> *intention to destroy or damage property belonging to another or*
>
> *recklessness as to whether such property is destroyed or damaged*

The aggravated offence comes under **s 1(2)** and is destroying or damaging property with intent to endanger life

S 1 (3) provides that destroying or damaging property by fire is charged as arson

Task 19

Apply the law on criminal damage to the facts of **Stringer 2008** and reach a logical conclusion as to which offence(s) he would be guilty of.

Concepts connections

Morals

Criminal damage allows a defence of lawful excuse. There may be times when it is morally right to cause damage e.g. where D believes the owner would consent or where it is necessary to protect other property. Also D's conviction or acquittal may be based on whether what D did is seen as morally acceptable.

Jaggard seems at odds with the rule that intoxication is not a defence to a basic intent crime.

Justice

As above, if D's conviction or acquittal is based on what is seen as morally acceptable then justice may not be served. Jaggard can be used here too, as can the note under fault below.

Fault

The low level of fault (objective recklessness) which used to apply to criminal damage was unjust. It is right that fault is based on D's own thoughts (subjective recklessness) not those of any 'reasonable person'.

Balancing conflicting interests

In anti-war demonstrations and environmental protests the individual's right to protest is balanced against community interests.

Creativity

Abolishing objective recklessness in **Gemmell & Richards** and shows the need for judges to be creative. The decision of the HL to use the practice statement to overrule its own previous decision was correct

Study Block 3: Defences

Chapter 9: Duress and duress of circumstances

Chapter 10: Intoxication

Chapter 11: Self-defence and the prevention of crime

This study block covers general defences. Unlike the specific defences (which only apply to murder) these apply to most offences. The summary at the end of this Study Block will compare the defences and the different effect of each for the person using them.

If you studied crime for Unit 3 you will have covered intoxication as well as self-defence and the prevention of crime, so use these chapters as revision.

Duress and duress of circumstances are used where D feels compelled to commit an offence because of a threat of some sort. There is an overlap between these defences, sometimes also referred to by judges as necessity, so I have included a brief word about that although it is not in the specifications as a separate defence.

Example

Harry tells Andy that if Andy doesn't rob a bank he will beat him up. This is duress. If Andy drives into another car because he is being chased by a gang threatening to beat him up, this would be duress of circumstances. Here the threat isn't directly from another person but from the circumstances Andy finds himself in. It could also be seen as necessity as Andy feels it is necessary to act as he does.

So, when discussing any possible defences, remember that you may have to discuss more than one when applying the law to a problem scenario.

Chapter 9 Duress and duress of circumstances

By the end of this Chapter you should be able to:

Explain these defences and the limitations on them

Distinguish between the defences, whilst noting the overlap between them

Explain how the law applies in practice by reference to cases

In these defences D is arguing that there was no alternative to committing the crime. It was necessary due to a threat, or to the circumstances. **Duress of threats** is where there is a specific threat of harm to D if a particular crime is not committed. **Duress of circumstances** is where there is also a threat of harm. However, here the threat comes, not from another person, but from the surrounding circumstances.

Example

Don tells Dave that if he does not rob a bank he will kill his family. Dave can use duress as a defence to a burglary charge.

Don finds that Dave's family are away so instead he says he will set fire to his house if he doesn't rob the bank. Dave can't use the duress defences here as there is no threat of harm.

Dave is attacked by a violent gang whilst waiting at the traffic lights. He jumps the red light to get away. Dave can use duress of circumstances to the driving offence.

The word necessity has been used somewhat interchangeably with duress lately. However they were distinct defences and you may see references to both. For this reason we will briefly look at necessity first and then look at duress in detail.

Necessity

There is some difference between necessity and duress. It is clear that duress cannot apply to murder, but necessity was used to justify a death in **Re A (Conjoined Twins)**. A hospital sought a declaration that it would be lawful to operate on Siamese twins in the knowledge that one twin would die. The operation was the only way to save the life of the other twin. As it was clear that one twin would die it there would have been an intentional killing, which could have been murder. The CA granted the declaration and also confirmed they would have a defence of necessity. The CA made a distinction between cases of duress by threats or circumstances, and cases of real choice. In the latter, the question is one of justifying a choice between two evils. This is the defence of necessity. It would only succeed where the act *was necessary to avoid an inevitable evil, and the evil inflicted was not disproportionate* to the evil avoided.

However, the dividing line between duress of circumstances and necessity, if any, is very faint and the terms have been used interchangeably by the courts. In fact in **Quayle 2005**, a new term, 'necessity by circumstances' was used.

In **Quayle 2005**, D had argued necessity in defence to a charge of growing cannabis. He argued that it was necessary for medical reasons. He was in pain and it was the only drug that allowed him to sleep without knocking him out. He did not want to take anything that knocked him out as he had children to look after. The CA rejected his appeal. They referred to the "defence of necessity where the force or compulsion is exerted not by human threats but by extraneous circumstances" adding that both "duress of threats and necessity by circumstances" should be confined to cases of threats of physical injury.

We will look at duress first, as this is where the rules were established. Then we can look at some cases to illustrate duress of circumstances. You should note however, that the rules have developed to cover both types of duress. In particular the HL reconsidered the whole issue of duress in **Hasan 2005** (duress of threats), and this was applied by the CA in **Quayle 2005** (duress of circumstances) with approval.

It is for D to provide evidence of duress, but then the burden of proof is on the prosecution to disprove it. If the defence succeeds then D will be acquitted.

Duress

The original defence of duress occurs where D is forced to commit a crime because of a threat. An example would be "if you don't steal the money, I will shoot you". It is sometimes called duress of threats. This is mainly to distinguish it from the more recently developed, duress of circumstances.

Key case

The test for establishing the defence was laid down in **Graham 1982**. D was a homosexual who lived with his wife and another man. He was charged with the murder of his wife. He alleged that the other man had threatened and intimidated him, and argued duress as a defence. The HL upheld his conviction and established the test for duress. It is a two-part question for the jury:

Was the defendant impelled to act as he did because he believed that he had good cause to fear that if he did not so act he would be killed or caused serious injury? If so have the prosecution made the jury sure that a sober person of reasonable firmness, sharing the characteristics of the defendant, would not have responded that way.

Put more simply:

> **Did D believe that there was good cause to fear death or serious injury if the crime was not committed – subjective**
>
> **would a sober person of reasonable firmness sharing the same characteristics have responded that way – objective**

The test is therefore in part subjective and in part objective. However, the first part is not fully subjective because D must have 'good cause to fear'. Unlike self-defence and mistake, where as long as a belief is genuinely held it need not be reasonable, for duress it must be a reasonable belief.

The threat

The threat has to be a serious one. Firstly, it must be a threat of *harm*. In **Valderrama-Vega 1985**, it was said that financial pressure and a threat of disclosing that D was a homosexual was not enough. In **Shayler 2001,** the CA said that duress was only available where the threat was to 'life or serious injury'. In **Wadsworth 2009** a woman pleaded duress to a charge of theft. She had stolen from the bank where she worked over a period of time, due to demands made by her boyfriend. She argued that she was in fear of violence and believed he would kill her or her family if she did not bring him the money. She had good cause to fear serious violence and the defence succeeded. However, in **Van Dao 2012**, the defence failed in a case where D had cultivated cannabis under threat of being held prisoner, as this was not sufficiently serious.

Secondly, the threat must be *imminent*. The rule was that if D could seek police protection or take evasive action then the defence was unavailable. Thus in **Gill 1963**, the defence failed because although there was a threat of harm if D did not steal a lorry, he had time to escape and seek help. This rule was relaxed in **Hudson and Taylor 1971**. Two young girls had lied in court because they were told they would be harmed if they testified against the accused. They successfully appealed against their conviction for perjury. The CA rejected the prosecution's argument that the threat wasn't imminent. They said that it was irrelevant that it could not be carried out immediately; it could be carried out on the streets late that night. The CA clearly recognised that the girls may not have received effective police protection from the threats. In **Abdul-Hussain 1999,** the Ds successfully appealed against a hi-jacking conviction. They believed they would be executed if returned to their own country, which they thought was imminent, and hi-jacked a plane to escape. The CA accepted duress of circumstances did not need an *immediate* threat, as long as it was *influencing* D at the time the crime was committed.

However, in **Hasan 2005**, Lord Bingham referred to both these cases and disapproved them on this point. He thought the limitation that D must have no chance of evasive action had been "unduly weakened". This HL case reaffirms that the threat must be immediate, or at least there should be no possibility of taking evasive action.

Key case

In **Hasan 2005**, D had fallen in with a drug dealer who was known to be violent. He told the dealer about a house where there was a lot of money kept in a safe. The dealer then told him that if he didn't burgle the house his family would be harmed. When charged with burglary he argued duress. Lord Bingham said that the defence was excluded where, due to a 'voluntary association' with criminals "he foresaw, or ought reasonably to have foreseen, the risk of being subjected to any compulsion by threats of violence". He also said that if the harm threatened was not "such as he reasonably expects to follow immediately, or almost immediately", then there was little doubt that D should take evasive action "whether by going to the police, or in some other way, to avoid committing the crime".

In **Hasan 2005,** Lord Bingham restated the essential requirements for duress. These are:

The threat relied on must be to cause death or serious injury

The criminal conduct which it is sought to excuse has been directly caused by the threats

The threat must be directed to D or a member of D's family, or to "a person for whose safety the defendant would reasonably regard himself as responsible"

D may rely on duress only if there was no evasive action that could reasonably have been taken (such as going to the police, disapproving Hudson & Taylor)

The questions for the jury were both objective (did D 'reasonably believe' there was a threat, approving Graham)

The defence is not available where, as a result of a voluntary association with criminals, D "ought reasonably to have foreseen" the risk of violence

Examination pointer

Look for any evidence of a threat in the given scenario. If there is a threat from a person then duress will be appropriate. You will need to apply each of the rules from **Hassan** to decide whether you think the defence will succeed.

Sober person of reasonable firmness

In **Graham**, D had been drunk as well as threatened but the court said that voluntary intoxication could not be taken into account. The test refers to a *'sober person'*. *'Of reasonable firmness'*, means factors such as timidity and susceptibility to threats will not be taken into account. In **Bowen 1996,** D had been charged with obtaining services by deception. He said he only did it after he and his family were threatened. The court refused to take his low IQ into account. However, as well as age and sex the CA did say that pregnancy, a recognised mental illness or serious physical disability could be relevant characteristics because these could affect D's ability to resist.

Self-induced duress

In **Sharp 1987** D had been involved in a plan with a gang to commit a robbery, he then tried to withdraw but was threatened. Someone was killed during the robbery and his conviction for manslaughter was upheld. The CA made clear that the defence would fail where D knew that the gang he had joined might put pressure on him to commit an offence. This is self-induced duress as D had a choice in the first place. The key issue is what is known about the gang. In **Shepherd 1987**, the defence succeeded as there was no evidence of any violence prior to the threats. It is now clear that this is an objective test. Even if D didn't know of any violent tendencies, the defence will fail if these would have been obvious to anyone else. This was made clear in **Hasan**, which is an example of self-induced duress. The question is whether D *should* have known, rather than whether D *did* know, that there was a risk of being threatened. The words "or ought reasonably to have foreseen" in **Graham** had indicated this.

In **Ali 2008**, D had been charged with robbery. He did not deny the robbery but said that another man had forced him into it. His parents had warned him the man was a criminal and to stay away from him. He pleaded the defence of duress. The CA held the defence was not available where, because of a voluntary association with others engaged in criminal activity, D foresaw, or 'ought to have foreseen', the risk of being subjected to any compulsion by threats of violence to commit criminal acts. If so the duress will be deemed voluntary and the defence will fail. The main question was whether he had voluntarily put himself in a position where such a risk was reasonably foreseeable, and it was made clear that this was an objective test.

Duress of circumstances

Duress of circumstances arose during the 80's in driving offence cases. Recognising that necessity was rarely allowed as a defence, lawyers had started to argue that duress could extend beyond the traditional 'threat by a person' to situations where D has no alternative but to commit a crime. In **Conway 1988,** D was in his car when he was approached by two men. He believed they were going to attack him and he drove recklessly to escape from the perceived threat. The CA accepted the defence and said it was 'convenient' to refer to such a defence as 'duress of circumstances'. In **Martin 1988**, D had driven his son to work whilst disqualified. He argued that his son might lose his job if he was late and his wife had threatened to commit suicide if he did not take him. The judge said that English law recognised a 'defence of necessity' in extreme circumstances. In such cases, where the threat came from dangers other than a threat from another person, *"it is conveniently called duress of circumstances"*. In the early days, it was most commonly used for driving offences. In **DPP v**

Bell 1992 D drove whilst drunk, again to escape from a threatening gang. The defence succeeded because as soon as he was out of danger he stopped in a lay-by. In **Mulally 2006**, a woman drove whilst drunk but was not in danger at the time, so the defence of duress was rejected. This shows that as with duress, the threat must be effective at the time of the crime or the defence will fail.

The defence is not confined to driving offences. In **Pommell 1995,** D was charged with possession of a firearm and successfully argued duress. He said that he had taken the gun from someone who was threatening to use it in a revenge attack. As this was in the early hours of the morning, he kept it overnight, intending to take it to the police in the morning. The police had, he said, arrived before he could do so.

Although coming from circumstances rather than a person, in all these cases there was a threat of physical harm, either to D or to another.

Examination pointer

If there is no evidence in the given scenario of a threat from a person, look for any circumstances that may be threatening, and consider duress of circumstances. There still needs to be a threat of physical harm, whichever defence is used. Duress of circumstances is more common, so apply the rules from **Hassan**. If there is any evidence that D belongs to a gang, look at how **Hasan** confirmed the rules on self-induced duress seen in **Sharp** and **Shepherd**.

Task 20

Look at the following situations and decide if I can successfully use a defence of duress, using a case in support:

> I am threatened with being exposed as a cheat and a drunk if I do not steal a packet of smoked salmon from the supermarket. I do so and am charged with theft.
>
> I am chased by a man who is threatening to hit me. I steal a car to escape. I drive to a nearby house where I have friends. I am charged with theft.
>
> I am at a party and a bit drunk. As I live 50 miles away I intend to stay overnight. An old enemy turns up and threatens to beat me up. I run outside and see my car in the drive. I get in and drive all the way home. I am charged with driving with excess alcohol.

Duress and mistake

Conway shows that D can use the defence even if there is no actual threat. It turned out that the people D thought were going to attack him were plain-clothes policemen. However, he was able to rely on duress even though he was mistaken as to the threat. He was judged on the facts as he honestly believed them to be.

In **Safi 2003,** the judge had suggested there had to *be* a threat but the CA said that this was wrong. They confirmed that the **Graham** test was still the law. Thus both types of duress could (as with self-defence) be used with mistake. However, there is a difference. With duress the mistake must be reasonable. This was implied by the test in **Graham** (did D have '*good cause to fear*'?) and has now been confirmed by the HL in **Hasan**. Lord Bingham said, "there is no warrant for relaxing the requirement that the belief must be reasonable as well as genuine".

Limits to the availability of the defence of duress

We have seen some of the limitations in the cases discussed. They were restated by the HL in **Hasan 2000**:

> Duress does not apply to murder – Howe 1987
>
> Nor attempted murder – Gotts 1992
>
> D may not rely on duress as a result of a voluntary association with others engaged in criminal activity where there was a foreseeable risk of being subjected to threats of violence – Sharp 1987

In **Wilson 2007**, a teenager was accused along with his father, of murdering his mother. He argued that he only helped in the murder because he was scared of his father. The CA confirmed that however much duress a person was under the defence was not available for murder.

In its **2006 Report (No. 304)** the Law Commission proposed that legislation should provide that the defence should apply to all offences including murder and attempted murder but these proposals have not been implemented.

Summary

Defence	Requirements	Limits
Necessity	The evil avoided is greater than the evil done	Case by case basis. Could justify a killing (**Re A**)
Duress	Imminent threat of death or serious injury (from a person) D had 'good cause' to believe such a threat (**Graham/Hasan**) a reasonable person would have acted as D did	Not murder or attempted murder (**Howe/Gotts**) Not where D voluntarily associates with those foreseeably posing a risk of threats No evasive action possible (**Hasan**)
Duress of circumstances	Imminent threat of death or serious injury (from circumstances) D had 'good cause' to believe such a threat (**Graham/Hasan**) a reasonable person would have acted as D did	Not murder or attempted murder No evasive action possible (**Hasan**) The threat need not come from a person but must be external to D (**Quayle**)

Self-test questions

In which case was the test for duress established?

What did **Hasan** confirm in regard to the first part of this test?

Is the test for self-induced duress an objective or subjective one?

What point was confirmed in **Quayle** about the source of the threat?

For answers to the tasks and self-test questions, please go to my website at www.drsr.org and click the button 'Answers to tasks'. For a range of free interactive exercises, click on 'Free Exercises' to see what's available.

Chapter 10 Intoxication

"If a man, whilst sane and sober, forms an intention to kill ... he cannot rely on this self-induced drunkenness as a defence to murder"

Lord Denning

By the end of this Chapter, you should be able to:

Distinguish between voluntary and involuntary intoxication

Explain how the courts treat different types of drug

Explain the difference between specific intent and basic intent

Show how the defence applies by reference to cases

Although traditionally this defence only applied to drink, it is now clear that the rules on intoxication apply to both drink and drugs. In cases involving drugs a distinction has been made between those which are commonly known to cause aggressive or dangerous behaviour and those which are not.

Key case

In **Hardie 1985**, D was trying to get his ex-girlfriend to get back together with him. She gave him a sedative (Valium) to calm him down and then left him in her flat. Whilst she was out, he set fire to it. He claimed that he could not remember anything after he had taken the drug. The CA allowed his appeal against conviction and held Valium was *"wholly different from drugs which are liable to cause unpredictability and aggressiveness"*.

Thus, 'unpredictable' drugs are treated in the same way as alcohol. With sedatives, the courts will apply a test of subjective recklessness.

Example

D is given anti-depressant drugs by his doctor. They make him feel sick and he doesn't eat for several days. Together with the pills, lack of food has the effect of making him prone to outbursts of violence. During one such period, he lashes out at someone and is charged with assault. He argues intoxication as a defence.

The question will be whether he was reckless, i.e., appreciated the risk that taking the drug would lead to such aggressive and unpredictable behaviour. If he was not told about any possible side effects then it is unlikely he will be seen as reckless. However, if the doctor had warned him to eat regularly to avoid any side effects then his defence will probably fail.

Intoxication is only a defence if it can be shown that due to the intoxication D was incapable of forming the necessary intent. This was established many years ago in **Beard 1920**. The rules for the defence differ depending on whether D was drunk voluntarily or not.

Involuntary intoxication

This would occur where D did not knowingly take alcohol or drugs. An example would be drinking orange juice which someone had 'spiked', e.g., added vodka to. The intoxication must do more than make D lose their inhibitions, though, it must remove *mens rea*.

Key case

In **Kingston 1994**, D was given drinks which had been laced with drugs. He was then photographed indecently assaulting a 15-year old boy. He admitted that at the time of committing the offence that he had the necessary intent, but said that he would not have acted in that way had he been sober. The HL overturned the decision of the CA and held that intoxicated intent was still intent. Intoxication is therefore no defence if the defendant had the necessary *mens rea*, even if it is formed whilst involuntarily intoxicated.

In **Allen 1988**, the CA made it clear that the intoxication had to be totally involuntary; not knowing the strength of what you are drinking would not be enough. D had drunk homemade wine not realising it was very strong. He then pleaded involuntary intoxication when charged with indecent assault. The CA held that he had freely been drinking wine, knowing it to be wine. It was therefore voluntary intoxication.

Voluntary intoxication: Basic and specific intent

The basic rule on intoxication is that it can provide a defence to crimes of specific intent but not those of basic intent. In simple terms, the distinction is this: if a crime can only be committed intentionally then it is crime of specific intent; if it can be committed with some other form of *mens rea*, e.g., recklessness, it is a crime of basic intent

Key case

This distinction was made in **Majewski 1977** where the HL held that intoxication could not negate the *mens rea* where the required *mens rea* was recklessness. Essentially getting drunk was seen as reckless in itself. D had been charged with an assault after a pub fight. He argued that he was too drunk to know what he was doing. The HL upheld his conviction and stated that evidence of self-induced intoxication which negated *mens rea* was a defence to a crime requiring specific intent but not to any other crime.

Example

Whilst drunk, Sue takes someone's bag and is charged with theft. This is a specific intent crime. Sue's intoxication defence can succeed if she can show that she lacked *mens rea*. The *mens rea* for theft is 'intent to permanently deprive' another. She might show that because she was drunk she thought it was hers and so she had no intent to deprive anyone else of it.

If she destroyed the bag, she could not use the defence to a charge of criminal damage. This offence can be committed by 'intending ... or being reckless as to whether property is destroyed'. The fact that this can be done by 'being reckless' makes it a basic intent crime.

The distinction seemed straightforward but some doubt was cast on it in **Heard 2007**. D had sexually assaulted a police officer whilst drunk and argued intoxication as a defence. He was convicted and appealed on the basis that the crime was 'intentionally' touching another person sexually and thus a specific intent crime. The CA held that basic intent could include intention where the *mens rea* was only for the act itself and nothing further, as here. Specific intent could include recklessness where the offence required *mens rea* for more than the illegal act itself, e.g., a consequence. The CA also noted that not all offences could be categorised as basic or specific offences as some had elements of both.

Examination pointer

The Law Commission (in its 2012 paper on insanity) said

> "We define specific intent offences as those for which the predominant mens rea is one of knowledge, intention or dishonesty, and basic intent offences as all those for which the predominant mens rea is not intention, knowledge or dishonesty (this includes offences of recklessness, belief, negligence and strict liability)".

This is what many judges and academics had interpreted **Majewski** as meaning, but **Heard** has introduced some doubt. If the issue arises in an examination scenario I would use the earlier interpretation and just mention briefly that **Heard** has cast some doubt on this.

In **Dowds 2012**, the CA held that voluntary, or self-induced, intoxication was not capable of establishing a defence. Although the case involved the special defence of diminished responsibility, the CA made clear that the rules on intoxication apply to all defences, and to intoxication caused by drugs or other substances as well as alcohol.

Note that if you plead intoxication to a specific intent crime then you will still be guilty of any related basic intent crime. If charged with murder, this would be manslaughter. If charged with **s18 Offences against the Person Act 1861**, the result would be a conviction under **s20**. This is because you are using intoxication to negate the *mens rea* of intention. **Majewski** shows, however, that you will still be deemed 'reckless'. If there is no related basic intent crime then D may be acquitted. An example would be theft.

Examination pointer

Look carefully at the facts and at *how* D became intoxicated. First decide if it is voluntary or not. If it is then use **Majewski**, if not then use **Kingston**. You may need both if the matter isn't clear. Look at the type of intoxicant; if it is a drug, you will need to look at the distinction made in **Hardie**, between drugs likely to cause aggression and sedatives. Taking unpredictable drugs is likely to be seen as voluntary intoxication.

Task 21

In **Lipman 1970**, D had taken LSD and hallucinated, he thought he was fighting snakes. He killed his girlfriend by stuffing a sheet down her throat. How would the rules on intoxication apply to a murder charge?

The 'Dutch courage' rule

What if D forms the required *mens rea* and *then* gets drunk and commits an offence? This may occur where D becomes intoxicated in order to summon up the courage to commit the offence. This is called the 'Dutch Courage' rule.

In **Attorney General for Northern Ireland v Gallagher 1963**, D decided to kill his wife. He bought a knife and a bottle of whisky. He drank the whisky and then stabbed her. The HL held that once a person formed an intention to kill then the defence would fail. Lord Denning made the main speech including the quote at the beginning of this Chapter. He also gave two examples of when intoxication might succeed. Firstly, where a nurse at a christening got so drunk that she put the baby on the fire in mistake for a log. Secondly, where a drunken man thought his friend, lying in bed, was a theatrical dummy and stabbed him to death. Lord Denning said that in both cases D would have a defence to a murder charge. This latter is not dissimilar to **Lipman**, where D thought he was fighting snakes and ended up strangling his girlfriend.

Lord Denning's examples show that intoxication and mistake are closely linked. We will deal with mistake separately but for the moment let's just look at the overlap.

Intoxication and public policy

Public policy is one reason why the courts will not allow intoxication as a defence. It is not in the public interest to allow people who get drunk and then commit an offence to be able to rely on intoxication as a defence. In **O'Grady 1987**, D hit his friend over the head in the mistaken belief that the friend was trying to kill him. Both of them were drunk at the time. He was convicted of manslaughter and appealed. The CA refused to allow the defence and said:

> "There are two competing interests. On the one hand the interest of the defendant who has only acted according to what he believed to be necessary to protect himself, and on the other hand that of the public in general, and the victim in particular who, probably through no fault of his own, has been injured or perhaps killed because of the defendant's drunken mistake. Reason recoils from the conclusion that in such circumstances a defendant is entitled to leave the court without a stain on his character".

In **Dowds 2012**, Hughes LJ said

> "... public policy proceeds on the basis that a defendant who voluntarily takes alcohol and behaves in a way in which he might not have behaved when sober is not normally entitled to be excused from the consequences of his actions".

Intoxication is usually seen with other defences, as it rarely succeeds alone. When revising this area also look at self-defence to see how the intoxication defence applies alongside this.

Summary

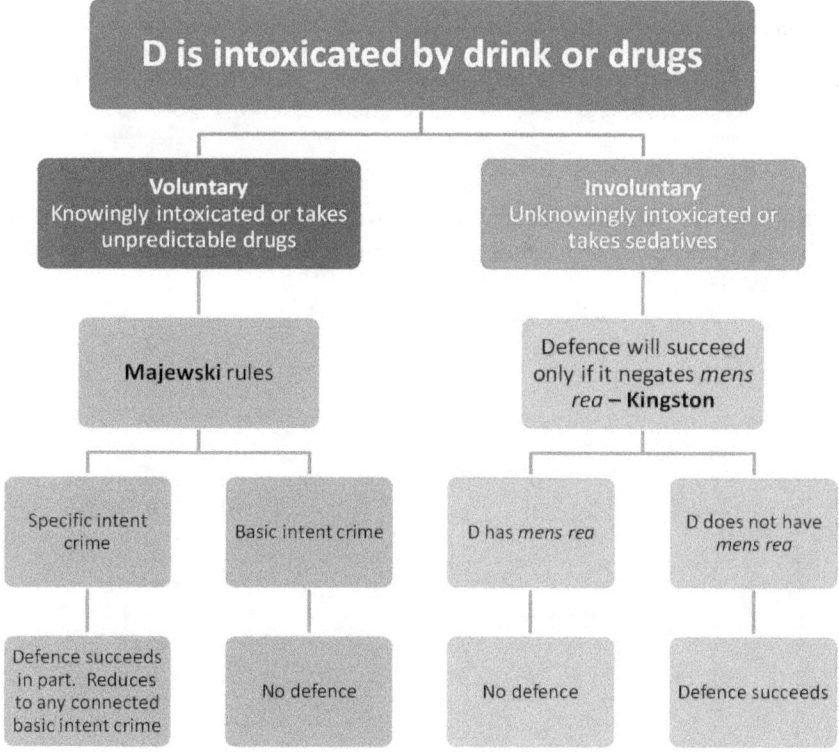

Self-test questions

What is the difference between specific and basic intent?

Name a crime for each type

What is 'Dutch courage' and will it provide a defence?

If D successfully pleads intoxication to a specific intent crime such as murder what is the result?

From which case did the opening quote come?

For answers to the tasks and self-test questions, please go to my website at www.drsr.org and click the button 'Answers to tasks'. For a range of free interactive exercises, click on 'Free Exercises' to see what's available.

Chapter 11 Self-defence and the prevention of crime

"... a person defending himself cannot weigh to a nicety the exact measure of his necessary defensive action"

The Privy Council in **Palmer 1971**

By the end of this Chapter, you should be able to:

- *Explain the defences of self-defence and prevention of crime*
- *Identify the principles on which these defences rely and how they overlap*
- *Refer to appropriate case examples*

The law allows a defence where D is doing something that would otherwise be an offence, but is acting to protect certain public and/or private interests. The term 'public and private defence' covers prevention of crime (public defence), self-defence, defence of another and defence of property (private defences). If successful, these defences result in an acquittal.

Prevention of crime

This is public defence. It is a statutory defence found in **s 3(1)** of the **Criminal Law Act 1967**, which provides that a person:

> "... may use **such force as is reasonable in the circumstances** in the prevention of crime, or in effecting or assisting in the lawful arrest of offenders or suspected offenders or of persons unlawfully at large".

The main point is that the defence is only available if the force used is *reasonable in the circumstances*.

Example

I see a man grab a woman and try to snatch her handbag. I pull him away and cause bruising. I can use **s3** as a defence if charged with battery. I was using 'reasonable' force to prevent a crime.

Self-defence

This is private defence. It is a common law defence developed by the courts. However many of the matters which have arisen are now covered by **s 76** of the **Criminal Justice and Immigration Act 2008**. Although usually referred to as self-defence, it covers force used in defence of another. In my example, I am also defending the woman, so could use self-defence as well as prevention of crime.

As seen in my example, the defences overlap, so the principles developed by the courts are essentially the same. In **Hitchins 2011**, the CA held that there was no difference between self-defence under the common law and **s 3**. **S 76** applies to both and is "intended to clarify the operation of the existing defences" in particular, as to whether the degree of force used was reasonable in the circumstances.

There are two main questions to consider:

Did D honestly believe the action was justified? (What D thought; a subjective question)

Was the degree of force reasonable in the circumstances? (What a reasonable person would do; an objective question)

The burden is on the prosecution to satisfy the jury that D was *not* acting in self-defence. They will have to convince the jury that in the circumstances, the action was *not* justified, or that *unreasonable* force was used.

Examination pointer

As with consent, self-defence is usually seen with the non-fatal offences against the person. For example, battery is the *unlawful* application of force. If D acted in self-defence and did not use excessive force, then the 'unlawful' part of the *actus reus* is missing. However, self-defence can apply to murder. The main issue would be whether killing someone was using excessive force. This will be a question for the jury based on the circumstances, or the circumstances as D believed them to be. If the person was armed and dangerous, that circumstance may justify extreme force. Note that if the defence succeeds D is acquitted.

Did D honestly believe the action was justified?

This subjective question is whether the particular D believed that the action which made up the offence was justified.

S 76(7) confirms the opening quote from **Palmer 1971**, stating that D "*may not be able to weigh to a nicety the exact measure of any necessary action*" and that if D only did what was "*honestly and instinctively*" thought to be necessary this would be strong evidence that only reasonable action was taken.

This means excessive force may be acceptable if D 'honestly and instinctively' thought it necessary in the circumstances. However, **s 76(6)** provides that the degree of force is not to be regarded as reasonable if it was disproportionate in the circumstances as D believed them to be. The force should not be disproportionate, but this is considered in the circumstances as D believes them to be; it is a subjective test. If D mistakenly believes someone is being attacked or threatened, then self-defence may be relied on, even if there was no actual threat. This was seen in **Williams (Gladstone) 1987**. A man saw a woman being robbed by a youth and struggled with him. D came on the scene and believed the youth to be under attack. He punched the man and was charged with actual bodily harm. His defence succeeded. The court held that he was to be judged on the facts *as he saw them*.

Was the degree of force reasonable in the circumstances?

This second question is objective and a matter for the jury to decide based on the circumstances of the case, and the nature of the threat. Early cases indicated that in order for the defence to succeed, D should show there was no possibility of retreat. However, in **McInnes 1971**, the CA said that a person is not obliged to retreat from a threat in order to rely on the defence, but that this may be evidence for the jury when considering whether force was necessary, and if so whether it was reasonable. As we saw above, **s 76(6)** provides that the degree of force is not to be regarded as reasonable if it was disproportionate. So D does not have to retreat, but if leaving the scene is an easy option then it may mean any force used isn't seen as reasonable.

There must however, be a perceived threat. In **Malnik v DPP 1989**, D had armed himself with a martial arts weapon and gone to visit a man whom he believed had stolen some cars. He was arrested when approaching the house. He argued that the man was known to be violent, so having the weapon to protect himself was justified. The court held that the defence was not available because there had been no imminent threat; he had put himself in danger by going to the house. Again, in **Burns 2010**, there was an easy alternative. A prostitute agreed to go with D in his car but later changed her mind and wanted to return to where he had picked her up. He tried to remove her forcibly from the car and she suffered cuts and bruises. The court held that he had used unreasonable force, which was therefore unlawful and a battery. It resulted in harm, so was ABH. The CA upheld his conviction and held the use of force was unjustified; he could have regained possession of the car simply by driving her back.

Example

I disturb a burglar in my house and, feeling rather brave, hit him over the head with a china vase. While he lies unconscious at my feet, I kick him in the ribs a few times to punish him for daring to enter my house. The first action may be self-defence. The second is not. There is no threat and I am merely exacting revenge.

In **Martin 2001**, the court confirmed that the test is objective and up to the jury to decide.

Key case

In **Martin 2001**, the jury rejected a plea of self-defence by a farmer who shot and killed a 16-year old burglar and seriously injured another. According to evidence, they were retreating and posing no threat, and the jury felt that using a pump-action shotgun was excessive force in the circumstances. In the CA, Woolf LCJ confirmed that the farmer was entitled to use reasonable force to protect himself and his home, but that the jury were *"surely correct in coming to their judgment that Mr Martin was not acting reasonably"*

Referring to the subjective and objective questions, he went on to say,

"As to the first issue, what Mr Martin believed, the jury heard his evidence and they could only reject that evidence, if they were satisfied it was untrue. As to the second issue, as to what is a reasonable amount of force, obviously opinions can differ ... it was for the jury, as the representative of the public, to decide the amount of force which it would be reasonable and the amount of force which it would be unreasonable to use in the circumstances"

S 76 states that the degree of force used by D was not 'reasonable in the circumstances' if it was disproportionate.

Mistaken use of force

Mistake is commonly seen along with self-defence in relation to the non-fatal offences against the person. It is where D uses self-defence mistakenly believing it is necessary in the circumstances.

Example

A man approaches me to ask directions. I mistakenly believe I am about to be attacked and hit him over the head with my umbrella. If I am charged with battery or actual bodily harm, the jury must decide if hitting him with an umbrella was justified in the circumstances that I believed, i.e., that I was being attacked.

Other than the above provision on disproportionate force, **s 76** states that what is reasonable is decided by reference "to the circumstances *as D believed them to be*", so there is a subjective element. If D is mistaken the jury must consider the circumstances that D believed, not the actual circumstances.

In **Williams (Gladstone) 1987**, above, D successfully argued self-defence based on his mistaken belief that his actions were justified because he believed he was defending the youth. In

Martin 2001, the defence failed because using a weapon was seen as unreasonable force, however Woolf LCJ confirmed that

"In judging whether the defendant had only used reasonable force, the jury has to take into account all the circumstances, including the situation as the defendant honestly believes it to be at the time, when he was defending himself. It does not matter if the defendant was mistaken in his belief as long as his belief was genuine".

In **Hargreaves 2010** (see GBH), D said that she had kicked out at her boyfriend as she believed he was going to attack her. This amounted to self-defence, because a mistaken belief can be relied on as long as genuinely held; she was not guilty of grievous bodily harm.

These cases, along with **s 76**, show that D may use mistake to justify the use of force even if it is not reasonable. The defence can succeed as long as D genuinely believes that force is justified in the circumstances.

Examination pointer

There are two ways to approach self-defence. Reasonable force can, for example, make a battery lawful, eliminating part of the *actus reus*, so there is no offence. Alternatively, reasonable force means self-defence can be used as a defence to a battery charge. Either approach is acceptable.

If a mistake is used to justify self-defence, you will need to discuss **Williams** as confirmed by **Martin** and by **s 76**, i.e., that the mistake must be genuine but does not have to be reasonable.

Self-defence and intoxication

Although a mistake need not be reasonable as long as it is genuine, an intoxicated mistake will not provide a defence. This is the case even though the mistake may have been honestly made.

In **O'Grady 1987**, D hit his friend over the head in the mistaken belief that the friend was trying to kill him. Both of them were drunk at the time. He was convicted of manslaughter and appealed. The CA rejected his appeal and said he could not rely on a drunken mistake to justify his actions. It was not fully clear whether this would apply to specific intent crimes such as murder, but in **Hatton 2005**, the CA said the rule applied whether the charge was murder or manslaughter. **S 76 (5)** confirms that D cannot rely on a mistaken belief caused by voluntary intoxication. Therefore, D can use the defence based on an unreasonable mistake, but not a drunken one.

Task 22

Discuss what defence(s) Amy should use in the following situations, using a case to support this and explaining whether it is likely to be successful and, if so, the effect it will have.

1. Amy is walking down the street one dark and rainy night when a young man steps out of a doorway right in front of her. Being a paranoid sort of person, she thinks she is being attacked and strikes out in alarm, cutting his cheek. In fact, he was just coming from his own house.

2. Walking home from the pub in a drunken haze Amy sees what she thinks is a man with a weapon coming towards her. She picks up a brick and hits him over the head, causing severe concussion and a nasty cut. It turns out he is from the local radio and is interviewing people on the streets for their views on violence at closing time.

3. Amy is walking down the street when she sees someone whom she believes is assaulting a young man. She intervenes and attacks him but he promptly arrests her. It turns out he is a policeman in plain clothes.

Examination pointer

You may need to explain and apply the rules on self-defence and mistake when assessing whether the force was justified. Explain that force must be reasonable but if it is then self-defence can, for example, make a battery lawful, therefore taking away part of the *actus reus*. If the facts indicate that D is acting under a mistake discuss the additional rules, i.e., that the mistake must be genuine but does not have to be reasonable. Finally if D is intoxicated use O'Grady to explain why the defence will fail

Summary of key issues

- Did D honestly believe that self-defence was justified? **Williams (Gladstone)**
- Was the force reasonable in the circumstances? **Martin**
- D is judged on the facts as they are believed to be, even if that belief is mistaken **Williams (Gladstone)/s 76**
- D cannot rely on a drunken mistake **O' Grady/Hatton/s 76**

Self-test questions

What are the two main questions for the jury?

Why was self-defence rejected by the jury in **Martin**?

Can you rely on a mistaken belief to justify using force?

What was decided in **Hatton** and confirmed by s 76?

What is the result of a successful plea of self-defence?

For answers to the tasks and self-test questions, please go to my website at www.drsr.org and click the button 'Answers to tasks'. For a range of free interactive exercises, click on 'Free Exercises' to see what's available.

Summary 3: Defences and their effect

This summary looks at the application of the defences. An important thing to note is the *effect* of the defences. This will help you decide which one is most appropriate in a given scenario.

Defence	Main points	Which crimes	Effect
Intoxication – involuntary	must remove *mens rea* – *Kingston*	All crimes requiring *mens rea*	Acquittal
Intoxication – voluntary	*Majewski*	Specific intent crimes	Reduces to basic intent crime
		Basic intent crimes	Guilty
Self-defence	force must be reasonable	All	Acquittal
Mistake	must be genuine but need not be reasonable	All	Acquittal
Necessity	limited defence	All	Acquittal
Duress	direct threat of imminent death or serious injury	Not murder or attempted murder	Acquittal
Duress of circumstances	threat of imminent death or serious injury by circumstances	Not murder or attempted murder	Acquittal

Task 23

Note the principle and brief facts of the following cases

Kingston

Majewski

Williams (Gladstone)

Graham

Hasan

Sharp

Quayle

Gotts

Concepts connections

Morals

The law on duress recognises that D may be morally justified in committing an offence, e.g., for fear of harm. However, duress is not a defence to murder, as killing cannot be morally justified – **Howe**.

Justice

The law on duress excludes D's vulnerabilities which can be unjust – **Bowen**

Balancing conflicting interests

The individual's right to be safe from harm has to be balanced against the community interest in being safe from crime

Fault

The rules on these defences recognise D is less at fault in that although *mens rea* is present, the offence is committed for a reason. The limits on the defence mean this is kept within strict bounds - **Hasan**

Examination practice

About the examination

These take place once a year in June. The last January exams were in 2013.

There are no essay questions for Paper 4A. It is important to know and understand the different statutes and their terminology. It is also important to know cases well as these have developed the law. Problem questions require you to use the current legal tests, which usually come from judicial decisions. Some crimes (including murder) are common law offences so *all* the law comes from cases, and even if the law comes from a statute, as with most property offences, that statute has to be *interpreted* by judges. Make sure you know the **Key cases** well as these are essential. You need to apply the law that is both current and relevant to the given facts. Only explain what is relevant to the particular circumstances. If you ask a solicitor for advice, they won't tell you everything they know, they will pick out the law that suits your case. You have to do the same in an examination question. Don't write down everything you know just to prove that you have learnt it. Being selective is a skill in itself. Use the **examination pointers** and **key cases**, plus the **diagrams** or **summaries** at the end of each chapter as a guide. An answer should be rounded off with a conclusion as to liability. This need not necessarily be a firm conclusion. It is unlikely to be clear-cut, especially in cases where a jury may be making the decision. In any case, never start an answer with "D will be guilty of ...." You need to show you can use and apply the law to reach a logical conclusion. Identify the appropriate area of law, apply the relevant rules, consider whether a defence is available and conclude along the lines of "D may therefore be charged with/ ..., but may be successful in pleading the defence of ..."

I will repeat what I said in the instruction here as it is important.

In precedent, you learnt that the important part of a case is the *ratio decidendi*, the reasoning behind the judge's decision. As you revise a case, think about this and look for the legal principle. Try to summarise the facts in a few words. It is valuable when it comes to exams and time is short. Don't be tempted to write all you know about the area. An examiner won't be able to give you marks for stuff that isn't relevant even if it is correct.

It is essential to:

Explain a case briefly but show that you understand the principle

Show that you understand the relevant law well enough to be selective

DO BOTH!

Examination pointer

Be clear that you are applying the specific law to the particular circumstances by frequent reference to the facts. This is a common complaint in examiners' reports, that candidates have clearly learnt the law but are unable to show they really understand it because of weak application to the given facts. The task below will help illustrate this.

Task 24

Look at the following short scenario and the two answers which follow. Explain why the second answer will be in the top band but not the first.

Fred took Jo's pay-as-you-go mobile from her bag and used it to call his mother in Australia because he was short of cash

Answer 1: Under s 1 of the Theft Act 1968, theft is the appropriation of property which belongs to another. This is the actus reus and it has been satisfied because Fred treated the property as his own to dispose of regardless of the owner's rights, as required by s 3 and it is clearly property under s 4 and it belongs to another as required by s 5 (and someone having possession of it is enough). Fred therefore has the *actus reus* of theft. As for the *mens rea* it must be shown that he was dishonest using the Ghosh test and that is probably the case here as most people would see it as dishonest, although there is a possibility the second part is not satisfied if he persuades the jury that he didn't realise this. It is also possible he could argue that he is not dishonest because s 2 provides three examples of when D is not dishonest and one of these is that D thinks the owner would have consented in the circumstances. This may be the case here. Finally, he must also have intention to permanently deprive. He has treated the property as his own to dispose of regardless of the owner's rights and this is enough to satisfy s6. However s 6 also includes using up the goodness (**Lloyd**). He has used up some of Jo's credit (which is intangible property under s 4) so subject to the dishonesty issue, he is guilty of theft.

Answer 2: Under s 1 of the Theft Act 1968, theft is the appropriation of property which belongs to another. This is the actus reus and it has been satisfied because Fred treated Jo's phone as his own to dispose of regardless of her rights, as required by s 3 and a phone is clearly property under s 4 and it belongs to another Jo, as required by s 5 – and even if it wasn't she had possession of it which is enough. Fred therefore has the *actus reus* of theft. As for the *mens rea* it must be shown that he was dishonest using the Ghosh test and that is probably the case here as most people would see using her phone without permission as dishonest, although there is a possibility the second part is not satisfied if he persuades the jury that he didn't realise this. It is also possible he could argue that he is not dishonest because s 2 provides three examples of when D is not dishonest and one of these is that D thinks the owner would have consented in the circumstances. Fred can argue he thought Jo would have consented as he needed to call his mother. It does not say but if Jo is a friend this is quite likely, especially if it was urgent for him to call his mother. Finally, he must also have intention to permanently deprive. He has treated the phone as his own to dispose of regardless of Jo's rights and this is enough to satisfy s6. However s 6 also includes using up the goodness (**Lloyd**). He has used up some of Jo's credit (which is intangible property under s 4) so subject to the dishonesty issue, he is guilty of theft.

Examination pointer

Remember that it is important to work logically through the *actus reus* and mens rea of the relevant offence. It not only improves your answer but also it will help you to reach the correct conclusion. Look back at Task 2 and the answer to this. What at first seems not to be theft because the property was put back in fact turns out to be by a logical application of the law.

Task 25 Application practice

In **Davies 2008**, Davies was convicted of several offences under the **Fraud Act 2006**. They were of two types. Firstly, he solicited contracts for building work and asked for a cash deposit but did not do the work. Secondly, he solicited investment funds, asking people to invest £633 on the basis it would produce a return of £1,000, but it actually produced nothing.

He had dressed smartly and called on people between the ages of 60 and 86 in their own homes. He put a lot of pressure on them, in some cases going with them to a cash machine to get the deposit. In some cases, he sought to cultivate their confidence by asserting Christian faith, which would make him trustworthy and in others he discussed his emotional difficulties to get their sympathy.

What offence has Davies committed? Apply the *actus reus* and *mens rea* of this offence to the facts and reach a logical conclusion.

Examination guidance

Before going on to look at a problem scenario here is some general guidance.

Read **all** questions carefully before deciding which to answer.

Look again at the scenario you wish to do to make sure you can answer the questions. Make a few brief notes; these can be a useful checklist later when you are tired and possibly short of time.

Structure your answer. Remember this is a test of **law** so you need to state the legal principles involved and apply them to the particular question. A solid start is worth a lot and gets the examiner on your side. As mentioned small plan is helpful.

Don't put in irrelevant material just because you know it – there is **never** a question asking you to 'write all you know about...'. The examiner wants to know that you understand the specific issues and can apply the appropriate law to the facts given. It is good policy to refer to the facts of a scenario as often as you can when applying the law as this indicates that you are answering the specific question and have a sound enough knowledge to know which cases are relevant to the particular facts.

Also on this point, you need to support your answer with **relevant** cases. Don't worry too much about the facts, the principle forming the *ratio decidendi* is usually the important part. There is no need to discuss the facts unless you want to show why you have chosen that particular case.

Example

In **West**, the court made clear that picking someone's pocket would be theft but not robbery. In **Clouden** wrenching a bag from someone was enough for robbery. If the scenario involves someone grabbing something from a person you might refer to the facts of **Clouden** to support your conclusion that this would amount to robbery.

If you can't remember the name of a case that is relevant don't leave it out but refer to it in a general way, e.g., 'in one decided case....' or 'in a similar case....'

Bear in mind that there are only a certain number of marks available for each question. The examiner has a schedule and so missing one half of a question and giving a brilliant answer to the other can only gain you half the possible marks. Planning your time is important.

Don't forget: Be logical in your approach to problem questions. Identify the various issues in the first paragraph and then set about dealing with them one by one by applying the relevant law to each issue, **referring to the facts of the question as you do so**. Then produce a logical conclusion based on your application.

Task 26 Application practice

Steve has a few drinks and for a laugh he grabs Jo's bag from her shoulder and throws it in the river. Steve said he grabbed Jo's bag and threw it in the river because his mates told him that if he didn't they would tell his parents he cheated in his exams. What offence(s) can he be charged with? Will he have a defence? Try this for yourself before looking at the sample answer and comments below. The comments on the answer are in bold and highlighted.

Sample answer

Robbery is defined under s8 of the Theft Act 1968. The first element of robbery is theft which is defined under s1(1) of the Act as the dishonest appropriation of property belonging to another. Appropriation, under s3, is the 'assumption of owner's rights', property, under s4, includes any 'money or other property, real or personal' and includes intangible property. The property is regarded as belonging to another when someone is in possession or control of it or has a proprietary interest in it. As in *Morris*, Steve (S) has appropriated Jo's (J) handbag which is property belonging to her.

This is correct but there is rather too much detail on matters that are obvious. A bag is clearly property and it says in the scenario it is Jo's. The main question is whether he appropriated it, as he did it for a laugh. The answer is that it is likely he has because although Morris was disapproved in part in Gomez, it was still made clear that an appropriation has taken place in such circumstances – so the issue of whether the appropriation amounts to theft will be one of *mens rea* not *actus reus*.

The first part of the mens rea for theft is dishonesty. S2 of the Act states three circumstances which make the defendant honest. These are belief the owner would consent, belief in a right to the property or belief that the owner could not be traced. None of these apply to this case and so the *Ghosh* test is applied. Was the defendant's act dishonest by the standards of reasonable and honest people? Did the defendant know his acts would be regarded this way by such people? It is likely ordinary people would regard this act as dishonest although there appears to be little malice in it and it was more of a practical joke. It is arguable whether the defendant realised his acts would be viewed this way the normal people.

The candidate says 'None of these apply to this case' so should have left out s 2 and gone straight to the Ghosh test.

Instead of 'It is likely ordinary people would regard this act as dishonest' it would be better to say 'It is likely ordinary people would regard taking Jo's handbag as dishonest'. Reference to the facts is important and shows the examiner you are sticking to the specific facts. Also, the conclusion conflicts with this statement though it is correct. It could be put more clearly e.g., ordinary people may not regard taking Jo's handbag as dishonest and even if they did it is unlikely that D realised his action would be viewed this way as he did it 'for a laugh'.'

S5 states intention to permanently deprive is the intention to treat the property as one's own to dispose of regardless of owner's rights. As in *Lavender*, S has treated J's handbag as if it were his own. In *Lavender*, it was arguable that he hadn't intended to permanently deprive the council of the doors as he merely moved them around, but the court held he had treated them as his own to dispose of regardless of the other's rights. This would be the same for Jo's bag which he has moved from her shoulder to the river.

This is good, though I would prefer the candidate to introduce this point, especially as it was not included in the earlier definition of theft. I would start by saying that the second part of the *mens rea* is the intention to permanently deprive and then continue with the definition in s 5 and the case example.

Robbery comes under s 8 of the Act and is theft with the use of or threat of unlawful force on a person. The force must be immediately before or at the time of the theft and it must also be in order to steal. In this case, S snatched the handbag, like in *Corcoran v Anderton*, which was at the time of the theft and in order to steal. The defendant must intentionally or recklessly use or threaten the use of force. In this case, the defendant was certainly reckless and has probably intentionally used force as he 'grabbed' the bag. It is clear from the above case and from *Clouden* that force can be minor and it is on a person as he grabbed it from her shoulder.

All elements necessary for theft have been satisfied, the only issue may be S's knowledge that his acts were dishonest by the standards of reasonable and honest people. Although the force requirement is also satisfied, if there is no theft there can be no robbery.

This is also much better than the earlier application as it is the correct law, logically applied and with good reference to the facts.

Voluntary intoxication, as distinguished in *Majewski*, can provide a defence to crimes of specific intent by mitigating the mens rea. However, if it is a basic intent crime, where recklessness will suffice, it doesn't provide a defence. The mens rea of robbery is either intentionally or recklessly applying or threatening the use of unlawful force. Recklessness is enough mens rea for robbery, so there is no defence of voluntary intoxication for S.

This may be true for robbery, but the defence can apply to the theft as theft is a specific intent crime – and if there is no theft there is no robbery.

The candidate did not discuss criminal damage. This can be a difficult paper in this way because so many offences overlap. Always be on the look-out for clues as to which offences and defences apply and try not to miss any.

The rules of duress were set out in *Graham* as a two part test. Was the D compelled to act because there was a good chance of serious injury or death? Would a sober person of reasonable firmness have been so compelled?

The defence is available if someone threatens death or serious violence against the defendant or another identified person unless the D commits a crime. As is *Valderrama-Vega*, the defence doesn't apply to S's case because it is not a threat of serious harm. It was confirmed in *Hasan* that the threat had to be of death or serious injury, a threat to tell his parents he cheated an exam is not enough of a threat so the defence would fail.

This final part is well explained and applied

Two main points arise in this answer which would need to be addressed to get in the top band.

The candidate discusses irrelevant matters in detail (as with property and belonging to another, and again with s 2). This will lose marks if it is at the expense of relevant matters (and anyway can bring down the A03 marks). Most importantly, it costs time. You should always try to stick to the main issues, but describe them accurately and apply the law logically with cases in support and with reference to the given facts of the scenario.

The second point is that you should always be careful to look for evidence of criminal damage. It is very often included as an issue with property offences (especially burglary where there may be a forced entry). Here it is needed with regard to damaging the bag by throwing it in the river.

Task 27 Application practice

As before try to answer this yourself before looking at the comments.

Tom was employed as a gardener by Enrique, a famous opera singer with a reputation for clean living. On his return to work after a lunch break in which he had drunk several vodkas at a local pub, Tom found a letter which had fallen from Enrique's pocket on to the garden lawn. The letter revealed that Enrique had been convicted many years previously of the rape of a young girl. Seeing Enrique in the garden Tom waved the letter at him and told Enrique that if he did not pay £10,000 for the return of the letter, Tom would sell it to a national newspaper.

Sample answer with comments

Blackmail is covered under s21 of the Theft Act 1968. It is a crime to make a demand, which is unwarranted, with menaces, with a view to gain for himself or another or cause loss to or expose another to the risk of loss. A demand can be made by words or by conduct. In this case, T had made a verbal demand.

A demand is unwarranted unless the defendant believes that he had reasonable grounds for making the demand and that the use of menaces was the proper means of enforcing the demand. If the defendant believes that at any moment he was acting improperly, as stated in *Harvey, Ulyett and Plummer*, the demand is unwarranted. In this case, T may have believed he had reasonable grounds for making the demand with E being a famous opera singer with a reputation for being good and it would therefore be in the public interest to know about E's previous rape of a young girl and T may also have believed that menaces was the proper way of enforcing this demand. However, it is unlikely that T believed this wholly and so the demand is likely to be unwarranted.

An unwarranted demand is said to be with menaces, as in *Clear*, if the victim is afraid, however *Garwood* made it clear that the demand can still be with menaces if an ordinary person of normal stability would be fearful, even if D is not. In this case, it is likely the T's unwarranted demand did make E fearful, especially as it is damaging to his clean reputation, and even if not most people would be fearful of such a threat, so T's demand for the £10,000 was with menaces.

The *actus reus* of blackmail is very well explained and applied, with good reference to the facts.

The mens rea of blackmail is that the unwarranted demand with menaces was made with a view to gain for himself or another or cause loss to or expose another to the risk of loss. In this case, T has made the unwarranted demand with menaces with a view to gain a sum of £10,000 for himself and also to expose E to a risk of loss (of his clean reputation). All elements of blackmail have been satisfied and a charge of this again T is very likely to succeed.

The *mens rea* is less well dealt with. The view to gain £10,000 is fine but the intent to cause a loss of his reputation would not be enough. Although the candidate gets the first part right the subsequent mention of the loss of reputation shows a lack of understanding of the *mens rea* requirement, which relates to money or property. S 34 (2)(a) provides that 'gain' and 'loss' are to be understood as *"extending only to gain or loss in money or other property.*

Voluntary intoxication can provide a defence to crimes of specific intent by negating the mens rea to that of basic intent. However, this defence is unavailable to crimes where recklessness (basic intent) is sufficient mens rea. In this case, T returned from the pub after several vodkas and therefore could have a defence to blackmail as this crime must be made with a view to gain or cause loss. T's mens rea for blackmail may be partially mitigated but it is unlikely the defence will succeed.

The discussion and application of intoxication as a defence is weak. The candidate did not even mention Majewski. It is necessary to explain the distinction between voluntary and involuntary intoxication, and then to use Majewski to further explain the distinction between crimes of specific and basic intent. The conclusion is also weak and somewhat contradictory.

Voluntary intoxication is a defence only to crimes of specific intent. Blackmail is an offence of specific intent because D must have 'a view to gain or intent to cause a loss'. There is no mention of recklessness in the Act, so the defence may apply. However, if it is to succeed Tom must show he was unable to form *mens rea*. Here it is arguable that Tom must have been able to form mens rea, he wasn't so drunk that he couldn't plan to blackmail Enrique so it is likely that he had intent.

Two main points arise in this answer which would need to be addressed to get in the top band.

The first relates to the explanation and application of mens rea. It should be made clear that there is no need for both a view to gain and intent to cause loss, therefore the view to gain £10,000 satisfies the mens rea requirement. Also note that there is no need to make any such gain (or cause any such loss), it is a matter of mens rea not actus reus, so as long as there is a view to gain or intent to cause loss this is enough to make out the offence.

Secondly the defence of intoxication needed a lot more explanation and application. Most candidates are able to explain the difference between voluntary and involuntary intoxication, and between crimes of specific and basic intent, but then have trouble applying the law. The main point here is that even though the defence can apply (because it is a specific intent crime) it is unlikely to succeed as he seems quite aware of what he is doing. As was said in Kingston, intoxicated intent is still intent.

For answers to the tasks and self-test questions, please go to my website at www.drsr.org and click the button 'Answers to tasks'. For a range of free interactive exercises, click on 'Free Exercises' to see what's available.

List of abbreviations

All these abbreviations are commonly used. You may use them in an examination answer, but should write them in full the first time e.g., write 'actual bodily harm (ABH)' and then after that you can just write 'ABH', similarly with the defendant (D) and the victim (V).

Case names should be in full the first time but can be shortened in later use if they are lengthy.

General

Draft Code – A Criminal Code for England and Wales (Law Commission No. 177), 1989

CCRC Criminal Cases Review Commission

ABH actual bodily harm

GBH grievous bodily harm

D defendant

C claimant

V Victim

CA Court of Appeal

HL House of Lords (now the Supreme Court)

SC Supreme Court (previously the House of Lords)

Acts

S – section (thus s1 Theft Act 1968 refers to section 1 of that Act)

s1 (2) means section 1 subsection 2 of an Act

OAPA – Offences against the Person Act 1861

OLA – Occupier's Liability Act

In cases (these don't need to be written in full)

CC (at beginning) chief constable

CC (at end) county council

BC borough council

DC district council

LBC London borough council

AHA Area Health Authority

Judges and other legal personnel (these don't need to be written in full)

J Justice

LJ Lord Justice

LCJ Lord Chief Justice

LC Lord Chancellor

VC Vice Chancellor

AG Attorney General

CPS Crown Prosecution Service

DPP Director of Public Prosecutions

AG Attorney General

Acknowledgements

I am grateful to the following for examination questions.

The Assessment and Qualification Alliance (AQA)

Note: Where worked solutions to, and / or commentaries on, AQA questions or possible answers are provided it is the author who is responsible for them. They have not been provided or approved by AQA and do not necessarily constitute the only possible solutions.

I am also grateful to my husband, Dave, for many hours of proof reading and for his hard work on the diagrams.

www.ingramcontent.com/pod-product-compliance
Lightning Source LLC
Chambersburg PA
CBHW060405190526
45169CB00002B/753